The Wit and Wisdom of an Ordinary Subject

Malcolm Watson

Soldier, Cricketer, Man of Letters

First published April 2013 using Lulu.com

9th Revise

© 2013 J M C Watson. All rights reserved.
IBSN 978-1-292-32095-4

In memory of my late mother-in-law,
Patricia Spooner,
who was incapacitated by a stroke
throughout the principal period covered in
this book, bar the first letter in January 2010
and the last, in April 2013.

FOREWORDS

Soldier

There is a wealth of wit and wisdom here that I have known and come to expect since first meeting Malcolm over 30 years ago. During a full career in the Army, he maintained many outside interests, and reading this splendid collection of letters I am full of admiration for the breadth, depth and scope of them. Not really an ordinary subject himself, he has left few of them unturned here and those concerning soldiering are as astute as ever. I look forward to *More …* and *Yet More Wit and Wisdom…* in the years to come.

General Sir David Richards GCB CBE DSO ADC Gen
Chief of the Defence Staff 2010-13

Cricketer

Malcolm once shared in an opening stand of 150 with Geoffrey Boycott at Pateley Bridge in 1973. As he informed me in a letter reproduced on page 140, it is surely the highest partnership ever recorded between two men who have had their spleens removed. This was unquestionably the most memorable nugget of useless information I received during my first year as editor of *The Cricketer*. It was also typical of the correspondent: witty, insightful and conveying the experience of a life well lived.

Andrew Miller
Editor, *The Cricketer*

Man of Letters

No publication worth its salt can manage without letter writers, those readers who apply a douche of common sense to each day's offerings. Drawing primarily on his submissions to the *Times* and *Telegraph* newspapers and *The Oldie* magazine Malcolm is one of that gallant breed who *knows*: that the Speaker's wife confessed to being a drunken ladette; about two-way roundabouts in Mexico City and how to compare beer and petrol prices. He can spot errors in the Court Circular, and reveals how the French greet him: "Ah! Sherlock 'olmes".

David Twiston Davies
Former Letters Editor of *The Daily Telegraph*

April 2013

CONTENTS

    Forewords

    Introduction   1

    Preface   3

1. Where it all began   5
2. 2010   9
3. 2011   21
4. 2012   73
5. 2013   159
6. Extras   191
7. The Last Word   199

    Acknowledgements   203

    About the Subject   205

INTRODUCTION

Prior to 2010, the two letters at the start of this book were the only ones I had ever had published. Then in March that year, an item in *The Daily Telegraph,* about bus drivers completing an obstacle course with fewer mistakes after they had had a glass of whisky, caught my eye and resulted in my first letter published there for 18 years. Not that I had troubled the editor many times in the intervening period, but since then I have written to a variety of other publications and gone from 6 successes in 2010, to 14 in 2011, 31 in 2012 and another dozen in the first quarter of 2013, when this collection ends.

Having now exceeded the 50 mark for published letters, I have some observations about the main recipients. First, with 5 letters published each year in *The Daily Telegraph* so far, I have come to the conclusion that some sort of quota system may operate for regular correspondents; with *The Times*, no such measure is evident – witness 10 entries in 16 weeks from 29 Sep 12 to 18 Jan 13. Secondly, *The Daily Telegraph* doesn't seem to touch anything serious I write about; *The Times* on the other hand publishes both my serious and, I hope, witty observations. Thirdly, with no successes in the period mid-July to mid-September each year, it appears that friendly sub-editors go on leave then and the periods provide rich veins of unpublished material. Lastly, if there is a formula for catching an editor's eye, then it is best encapsulated in this extract from a letter I found in *What's Brewing:* "… a successful letter is like brewing a good beer. It needs to be clear, have something to make it stand out from the others and a carefully monitored Original Brevity". Above all the subject matter must still be topical.

A number of friends and relations who have seen my efforts have not only encouraged me to keep writing, but to publish them as well. So here you have it, a compilation which includes most of the unpublished letters in addition to those already published in a format small enough to carry around and at a low enough price to give as presents, or download in a PDF format.

I hope you enjoy reading this book as much as I have in writing and compiling its contents, and that you find something in it which lives up to the title.

Malcolm Watson

Welford
Berkshire

April 2013

PREFACE

Published letters that follow are in a larger font to distinguish them from the others which were unpublished and in a smaller font. Both have the subject heading in bold.

The letters, or other submissions, are shown in date order as a reminder of some of the issues of the day. The dates shown are the date of publication, or the date of submission for those not published. Dates shown as references are in the format used in each publication.

The titles *The Daily Telegraph* and *The Sunday Telegraph* have been abbreviated to *DTel* and *STel* for unpublished letters and the definite article dropped for published ones to save space. Salutations, where they appear, are as used in the individual publications.

All letters have been signed: Malcolm Watson, Welford, Berkshire, except where shown.

Rank has only been used when writing on military matters to give credibility to the points at issue, though where this is not the case the connection might have been edited out.

Letters published in *The Times* under the picture and subject of the day are shown in bold type, as in the newspaper; those published in the *Telegraph* newspapers under the picture have (P) after the title. In all cases, the actual title of published letters is used, which will be that for the group of letters, when there was more than one.

THE WIT AND WISDOM OF AN ORDINARY SUBJECT

Where some letters seem to be repeated at later dates, they have been included to demonstrate the determination to get the subject aired. When such letters were sent to different publications at roughly the same dates, they are shown together as a single entry.

Entries in italics are from other sources or notes by way of explanation.

WHERE IT ALL BEGAN

Daily Telegraph 16 March 1992
Sports Letters

Man of Honour

SIR – David Gower states (March 5) that there is no particular honour in being the adjudicator of the man of the match in international cricket matches. In which case I should like to declare my availability for this summer's matches in England, except at Lord's and Headingley where I am a member.

Lt Col J M C WATSON
The Queen's Own Hussars
Wareham, Dorset

Mexico City Times　　　　　　9 May 1997

Leading A Dog's Life With Grammar

Dear Sir:

I read with interest your Joy of Spanish article today (Dog-Eat-Dog, 6 May). I have been learning Spanish since September last year and have asked my teachers, both in England and now here, how does one say, "My dog likes me". The answer appears to be, "Yo le gusto a mi perro", but apparently it is not, and should not be used. Can you help me?

Yours faithfully,
J. M. C. Watson
(Colonel, British Army)
Zacatecas

P.S. I do not have a dog, but me gusta aprender la gramática Española!

The answer to my question was published in the Mexico City Times two weeks later and took up 32 column-inches.

2010

DTel **Am I still alone?** 1 Jan

SIR - I wonder if any of your other readers have been disappointed not to receive a copy of *Am I Alone in Thinking…? Unpublished Letters to The Daily Telegraph* for Christmas. I had hoped to see if any of the witty, perceptive and knowledgeable letters I had sent you over the years had made it into print at last. I shall now be pinning my hopes on my birthday in February.

Private Eye **Commentatorballs** 20 Jan

"Stationary traffic is coming out of Manchester."
SALLY "TRAFFIC" BOAZMAN, Radio 2

Daily Telegraph 20 Mar

Driving after a drink

SIR - One reason why the bus drivers in the documentary (Letters, March 18) achieve better times on an obstacle course, without making any mistakes, after drinking a large whisky is that alcohol relieves stress.

This effect is well known to moderate skiers who ski much more fluently in the afternoon.
Col Malcolm Watson (retd)

DTel **English morals** 9 Apr

SIR - To a reply from the young "I'm good" (Letters 9 March), I have adopted the line "I wasn't asking about your morals, I was asking about your health." Result: puzzled smiles.

DTel **Dream ticket** 18 Apr

SIR - With the Lib Dems' shadow chancellor already well regarded widely amongst the electorate, are we seeing the emergence of Nick Clegg and Vince Cable as the first dream ticket in elections over here? Over there, one part of a ticket can also sink the other.

Daily Telegraph 21 Apr

The senseless notion of "zero tolerance" of volcanic ash in the atmosphere (P)

SIR - Perhaps the ash will enrich our land. Soil around the slopes of Popocatépetl is amongst the most fertile in the region and the produce grown there helps feed Mexico City's 23 million population.
Jane Watson

DTel **Value and standards – lowest common denominator** 24 Apr

SIR - Cameron no morning suit, Brown no tie. What next? Clegg only has to keep shaving...

DTel **Numbers of voters** 4 May

SIR - If such a distinguished newspaper as *The Daily Telegraph* thinks that "Fewer people in Britain bother to vote than in Sri Lanka or Malawi" when compared to the higher proportions voting in the much smaller populations of those countries, then we are indeed all doomed. (Letters, 3 May).

Daily Telegraph 25 May

Clichés do not take into account minor public schools

SIR - Public schools are not always *top* (Letters, May 24). Some are *minor*.

DTel **Keeping one's head** 26
May

SIR - It could also be that he who keeps his head whilst all around might be losing theirs (Leading Article, May 26) may not be fully in the picture.

Daily Telegraph 1 Jun

A drinking test

SIR - If binge drinking is defined as consuming the equivalent of four pints of beer in one day (report, May 27), then some of those who enjoy a day at the Test match at Lord's are binge drinking.

I don't think so. Spread over the day at an outdoor event this represents drinking

sensibly to many, whatever their class (Letters, May 28), or rank.
Col Malcolm Watson (retd)

Private Eye   **Commentatorballs**   5 Jun

"There's a word trying to limit peoples' salaries and it's called a pay policy."
DIANE ABBOTT, BBC Question Time.

DTel   **Contradictory signs**   30 Jun

SIR - There used to be two signs on a wall of the Lamb at Hindon. One was circular proclaiming "Coaching inn since 1642"; alongside was a rectangular sign, perpendicular to the wall, warning "NO COACHES". I miss them.

DTel   **Cricket redundancies**   28 Aug

SIR - The Chairman of the England and Wales Cricket Board (ECB) is reported to have said (Sport, August 27) that a reduction in cricket will mean redundancies, the inference being amongst the first-class counties. For the Test match at Lord's, 12 England players and a management team of 13 were permitted to enter the dressing room. Perhaps the "coalition" that constitutes the ECB should be looking to reduce the England management team in "fairness" to the counties.

DTel **Other bouncers** 23 Sep

SIR - I wonder what Harry Flashman, the notorious bully from Tom Brown's Schooldays, would have made of the fuss about the description of "bouncers". (News, September 23).

The Oldie **Ed's letter –** 24 Oct
advertising inserts

SIR: I have been buying and enjoying *The Oldie* since the August issue this year and was toying with taking up one of the subscription offers each copy contained. Imagine my delight when an advertising "insert" arrived inside my November copy of the *Wisden Cricketer* magazine offering 12 copies of *The Oldie* for £12 and a free *Oldie* cartoon book. The offer, which I have taken up, is better than anything so far seen in the *The Oldie* magazine itself. I note that the "inserts", or junk mail, complained about by readers, play a vital role in *The Oldie's* financial ecosystem and benefit miscellaneous charities, but doesn't charity begin at home?

THE WIT AND WISDOM OF AN ORDINARY SUBJECT

DTel **Dreaming written words** 27
Oct

SIR - One indication that intense foreign language training is succeeding is that you start dreaming in the language. I seem to recall that this included the written word (Letters, October 21), at least in the form of vocabulary lists and textbook titles such as "500 Spanish Verbs". Or am I dreaming?

The Times **Oxfordesque adjectives** 3 Nov
for batting

Sir, I read with the greatest interest and admiration the full range of adjectives used by John Woodcock in describing famous batsmen, past and present (Sport, Nov 3), without recourse to the superlative that most of us use when offering our views on the "best" batsman ever. I have seen in person all the players mentioned who were still playing in 1961 and since, and held that the best batsman I have seen live is Garfield Sobers.

Having consulted my dictionary, what I meant was the most "complete", but this is reserved for Barry Richards; most "expansive" is used for Sobers and I am content as its definition includes "able, extensive and comprehensive".

But it is not all down to being eye-catching and few, if any, will disagree with Mr Woodcock, when he says that Tendulkar is the Bradman of today. The final test may be whether "Tendulkaresque" joins "Bradmanesque" in cricket's lexicon.

DTel　　　　　**Sovereign choices**　　　　11 Nov

SIR - If an Act can be passed to rescind or repudiate any provision of the Treaty of Rome (Leading Article, November 11), then presumably the same applies to France. Does this account for why the French apparently chose to ignore some EU edicts?

   Perhaps the judicious use of the fact that you can legislate to make such action legal is sufficient to avoid the time and cost of doing so, for the same beneficial outcome.

DTel　　　　　**Strictly - the end?**　　　　26 Nov

SIR - Assuming Ann Widdecombe does not actually win the final of *Strictly Come Dancing*, all the remaining seriously good dancers will still leave in turn, but one programme early (Letters, November 26).

   If she wins, then perhaps the watching public are indicating that it is the show in its present format that is the joke, which by then will have strictly run its course.

The Oldie   Dec issue

Caught out

SIR: I enjoy reading James Hughes-Onslow's column on memorial services, but I do like accuracy. In respect of Sir Alec Bedser, Mickey Stewart was never captain of England, though he was sometime manager and coach; Sir John Major did not choose a piece of Oval turf as his luxury on *Desert Island Discs*, but a replica of the Oval ground and a bowling machine; Arthur Morris is not the sole survivor of the first Australian side which toured with Bradman after the war - Neil Harvey at 82 and Sam Loxton at 89 are also still alive.

Daily Telegraph   17 Dec

Variations on the elegant art of turning over in bed (P)

SIR - Using a headbutt to aid folding my copy of the *Telegraph* would risk injuring my head and breaking the screen of my laptop (Letters, December 15). One finger on the mouse pad is all that is required.

DTel **The wonder of estimating** 21 Dec

SIR - The BAA Chief Executive, Colin Matthews, states on BBC News that "something like" 30 tons of snow had to be lifted from under each aircraft on "something like" 200 stands at Heathrow airport. No wonder he had to admit that they had underestimated the task then.

DTel **Downturn Savoy** 22 Dec

SIR - Did anyone else notice that Hugh Boneville, who played the Earl of Grantham in Downton Abbey, narrated the two-part television programme about the re-launch of The Savoy hotel? What a downturn.

DTel **Letter mania** 28 Dec

SIR - In the interest of safety, please could you refrain from publishing any more of my father's ramblings to *The Daily Telegraph* (Letters, March 20, April 21, May 25, June 1, December 17). He takes much pride in framing and hanging each one of them, but I now fear

for the stability of the wall. I can only thank you for not publishing any more of his in the two books of your unpublished letters he gave himself for Christmas.
Fenella Watson

DTel **The Ashes – as they were intended** 29 Dec

SIR - Now that we have deservedly retained The Ashes for the first time in a generation, can we now set about regaining them for the English language as well? Surely the term should not be used as an adjective as in an "Ashes" Series or 4th "Ashes" Test, with all the associated hype, but solely as the name of the trophy played for between England and Australia in qualifying series of Test matches. If the Australians wish to use it as a brand name in their next campaign, so be it, but we will understand how desperate they have become.

The Times **The greatest glory** 30 Dec

Sir, Not so, Mr Brotherton (letters, Dec 30). The greater glory will be to retain The Ashes by winning the series - there is one Test match to go. The greatest glory is to regain them in Australia

.

2011

The Times 1 Jan

Fish with a kick

Sir, A Bloody Mary is made with vodka (times 2, Dec 30). Tomato juice and gin is known as a Red Snapper.

The Times 4 Jan

A merry old soul

Sir, A Red snapper (letter, Jan 1) is the original name for the vodka and tomato juice-based cocktail devised in the King Cole bar of the St Regis Hotel in New York. It is still called a Red Snapper in the St Regis.
CAROL MacDOUGALL
Glasgow

Private Eye **Commentatorballs** 3 Jan

"Billy the Trumpet has learnt a new tune and he's going to be playing it throughout the day at some stage."
DAVID LLOYD, 5th Test, Australia, Sky Sports

2011

DTel   **Brazen Hussey**   8 Jan

SIR - How intriguing to read that Mike Hussey's company is to be the preferred private partner in the redevelopment of Lord's cricket ground (Business, January 8). As their heaviest run scorer and the only Australian player who would get into the current England test team, the Marylebone Cricket Club will no doubt be hoping for an equally weighty contribution from his namesake towards the £400m scheme.

DTel   **Impish behaviour**   12 Jan

SIR - My Hillman Imps, Singer Chamois and Hillman California of the 60s and 70s all had to have their water pumps replaced (Letters, January 11), one in Tangier on the way back from skiing with a friend in the Atlas Mountains in April 1971. The only other setback on the trip was leaving a tin of Army "compo" marmalade in a cafe in Algeciras on the way out - essential for breakfast for some of us, then and now (Leading article, January 12).

The Oldie   **Shameful**   13 Jan

SIR - I switched on Sky News around midnight recently to find Mrs John Bercow commentating live as a Labour Activist and asking of bankers: "Do they have no shame?" Even if there was a late night sitting, does this self-confessed drunken ladette with a young family have no shame herself?

The Times **Best buys** 15 Jan

Sir, Jane MacQuitty is being disingenuous when she suggests two Robert Modalvi wines at £6.16 from Wednesday at Sainsbury's amongst "This week's best buys" (Weekend, Jan 15), when Majestic has had three of their wines available for £3.99 since last Tuesday. Or is she expecting them all to have been snapped up by Wednesday, as seems likely having tried to buy some?

DTel **Number not recognized** 22 Jan

SIR - Southern Electric Contracting may be one organisation that is not always busy on the telephone (Letter, January 22). Invited to ring the telephone number given on the back of one of their vans to comment on their driving, my call was answered with: "The number you have dialled has not been recognised. Please check and try again." I have been trying and checking ever since, but I suppose it's been the weekend.

| *DTel* | **Virtual mirrors** | 29 Jan |

SIR - Julie Capper shouldn't have found her virtual form on display at Manchester Airport strange at all (News, 29 January). As her image has been produced the wrong way around, it will have been as familiar as seeing herself in a mirror.

| *DTel* | **NHS investigative failures** | 2 Feb |

SIR - I fear that the experiences of the Ullyatt family with the hospital in Sheffield are not unique (News, February 2). In March last year, my wife submitted a formal complaint when staff on the stroke ward at Salisbury District Hospital were found feeding her mother, who was also Nil-by-Mouth.

Nine months of correspondence with the Chief Executive of the hospital has produced a plethora of apologies for what happened, but no convincing reason for why it did. At a meeting before Christmas with the newly appointed Interim Chief Executive, he acknowledged that the quality of their investigations was variable and that it was something he would strive to improve.

Having been involved some years ago with the submission of a Board of Inquiry into a serious failure in a British military hospital in West Germany that went all the way to the Treasury Solicitor, I have been astonished to discover that the NHS appears not to have any national regulations and guidance on the conduct of investigations into complaints, which in cases of Nil-by-Mouth are uncomplicated. It is high time that their investigations were carried out in a more rigorous, timely and robust manner. They could start by consulting the Defence Medical Services.

Sunday Times **Mad man?** 9 Feb

It would appear that Matt Rudd need only have addressed his stiff letters about advertisers' wild promises to Dear Madam (Magazine, February 20, pages 42-47).

The Oldie **Caught out – again** 11 Feb

SIR: Your reviewers (March) seem to be all at sixes and sevens. Marcus Berkmann (Film) could have told Christopher Andrew (Books), for his review of Keith Jeffrey's history of MI6 that it was King George V, not George VI, who was alleged to have died with the words "Bugger Bognor!". Berkmann himself didn't seem to notice in *The King's Speech* that Lionel Logue's "scabby little consulting rooms in a basement somewhere" were shown to be in Harley Street. For Valerie Grove (Radio), in the Tony Hancock episode, *The Bowmans*, the entire village was not blown up a by a landmine, though half of them did fall down a disused mineshaft.

| *The Times* | **Olympic tickets** | 15 Feb |

Sir, I wonder if any of your other readers have not found an Olympic event (London 2012, The Venues) that they would want to see at a ticket price that they would be prepared to pay.

| *DTel* | **Final decisions** | 22 Feb |

SIR - When I was serving in our embassy there in the late 80s, it used to be said that there was no such thing as a final decision in Washington. There is, of course, nothing more frustrating than having decisions overturned by factors that were not considered at the time, or if they were , not given due weight. Can this now be said of decisions over here what with school buildings, forests and now Harrier and Tornado?

| *Private Eye* | **Pseuds Corner** | 22 Feb |

"(Joanne) Trollope's forensic eye is at its steadiest as she traces the shifts of a family's tectonic plates - volatile material that depends on telling detail and convincing texture to anchor it.   Plot is not the point of this novel, but necessity of negotiating "emotional scar tissue" left by seismic shocks and contrary feelings is".

ELIZABETH BUCHAN reviewing the novel
Daughters-In-Law by Joanne Trollope in *The Sunday Times*, Culture section

Daily Telegraph 2 Mar

Petrol cheaper than beer

SIR - At the time of decimalisation it was still possible to get a pint of beer for 10p, or a gallon for 80p; a gallon of petrol was 33.3p. Compared to today's prices of £24 and £6 (Letters, March 1), beer now costs 30 times more, but petrol only 18 times more. Average earnings have gone up 20 times since 1971.

So it appears that petrol is not that expensive, while beer certainly is.

DTel **Cinematic one-liners** 3 Mar

SIR - "I run a couple of newspapers. What do you do?" *(Citizen Kane).* I write to them.

2011

Evening Standard   **Wanted – sock**   7 Mar

What is wanted for London's most wanted shoe, however it is described, is a sock (Trends, March 7).

DTel   **What not wear**   8 Mar

SIR - I am surprised that no one has yet admitted to not wearing trainers; I certainly haven't. Of course I have never worn jeans or a shirt with a buttoned-down collar either, but I invariably wear a hat.

The Times   **Double exposure**   10 Mar

Sir, The automatic acknowledgement of emails to your letters department includes the sentence "Letters must be exclusive to *The Times*". Twice this week letters you have published have also appeared in *The DailyTelegraph*, the first from David Fall giving credit to the Duke of York and the second from Katy Mitchell concerning retirement pay. It is difficult to see how this stricture can be enforced on those submitting letters for the first time. For the rest, the chance of double exposure will normally be so small that it is presumably worth risking multiple addressees. Congratulations to them both.

THE WIT AND WISDOM OF AN ORDINARY SUBJECT

Private Eye   **Commentatorballs**   11 Mar

"Bangladesh need 12 runs from 19 balls; three 4s, one 6."
DAVID LLOYD, England v Bangladesh, Sky Sports, ,

DTel   **God save us**   19 Mar

SIR - Not only does the England rugby team not know the words of the National Anthem, the BBC News clip on Saturday night then showed them singing a line they get wrong.

DTel   **Cost of stamps**   5 Apr

SIR - In comparing the prices of petrol and beer with the 20 times increase in average earnings since 1971 (Letters, March 2), it appeared that petrol was not that expensive while beer certainly was. A first-class postage stamp has now gone up by just over 15 times in the same period, which doesn't seem to be "ridiculously high" as suggested (Letters, April 5).

In stark contrast, a £2 bottle of wine in 1971 only costs 5 times more now, which might even be ridiculously low, though I won't be complaining.

The Times   **Best thing since**   2 Apr
before sliced bread

Sir, The name of William Oughtred, the inventor of the slide rule, is an inspired suggestion for a new prestigious engineering award (letter, Apr 12). Present-day Oughtred descendents are the biggest suppliers of sliced bread to the sandwich market in Europe through the family business, the William Jackson Food Group. The business also invented the frozen Yorkshire Pudding, which they sell under the *Aunt Bessie's* brand. Who knows, a sponsor for the award maybe ready in the wings!

Sunday Telegraph   7 Apr

Maths for the future

SIR - Bruce Denness is right (Letters, April 10). It is time to remind ourselves how essential mathematics is. All buildings, bridges and machines, whether operating on land, sea or in the air, are all based on maths.

The future is not sustainable without it, or those who understand and can apply it.

THE WIT AND WISDOM OF AN ORDINARY SUBJECT

Sunday Times　　　**The £5 bottle of wine**　　　18 Apr

There may well be merit in sticking up for the £10 bottle of wine (India Knight, April 17) - but only when it is on offer at a discount of 50%, as many often are.

DTel　　　**Chris Huhne and votes against**　　　19 Apr

SIR - Chris Huhne was vociferous and repetitive on Monday's *Newsnight* that votes not cast for a sitting Conservative MP with less than 50% of the vote, were votes cast against him. This myth must not be allowed to persist by remaining unchallenged. Votes are positive and if not cast for the elected MP they are cast for another candidate. Such votes are not negative entities. That is the whole point of first past the post - vote for whom you want to be elected and accept that the winner has the most votes. The possible distortion that emerges when there is a large number of candidates is supposed to be offset by the risk of a candidate losing their deposit. It would appear that it has not been set high enough in recent memory.

2011

DTel   **Costly getaway**   21 Apr
            or forecourt robbery

SIR - I have twice within recent months filled up my car with petrol using pumps at different stores of a well-known supermarket chain. The fuel tank takes 60 litres and both times the pump showed over 63 litres. My complaints at the checkouts elicited refunds and an assurance that the matter would be reported. I do not know whether the pumps were cordoned off until they were recalibrated, nor did I receive any feedback. This has happened to me only once before, 10 years ago, when the garage proprietor did not accept my complaint.

  It is virtually impossible to gauge whether a pump is correctly calibrated unless the tank is filled from nearly empty, but in these straightened times, motorists would be advised to do just that, if they want to ensure that they are not subject to fraud, inadvertent or otherwise, on top of already high fuel prices (News, April 21).

The Times   **Caring for patients by nurses**   24 Apr

Sir, Andrew Martin is right that we must be clear about the time nurses can allocate to bedside care of patients (letter, Apr 23). It is that part of their responsibilities - towards the daily essentials when they are confronted with them - which is not meeting reasonable patient expectations.

Increasing anecdotal evidence suggests that nurses are either not setting the examples expected of their degrees and hands-on training, or they are neglecting their responsibilities in favour of less well remunerated and qualified carers.

Leadership in this, as in all other professions which practitioners claim to be passionate about, starts at the top and not at the bottom, whatever the perceived constraints.

DTel **Duckworth/Lewis** 26 Apr

SIR - If anyone believes that the short explanation given by Messrs Duckworth and Lewis, as reported in Oliver Brown's article (Sport, April 21), is sufficiently detailed for potential AV voters to understand the target score in rain-affected (not "rained-off") cricket matches (Letter, April 26), then I suggest sticking with First-Past-The-Post.

The Cricketer **The real 1955** 27 Apr
heavyweight champions

The combined Yorkshire/Surrey team of England players chosen from the momentous season 1955 (Openers, *TWC*, May) is rather misleading, as Stewart and Illingworth had not yet played for England. However, replacing them with Yardley (like Hutton, also in his last season), Loader, Lock and Wardle, produces a squad which could have taken on the rest of England under all conditions.

DTel **Timely heirs to the throne** 2 May

SIR - Queen Victoria did not give birth to a son nine months after marrying Prince Albert in 1840, but a daughter, Victoria, (Features, May 2), who was heir to the throne until her brother Albert (later King Edward VII) was born the following year.

It is difficult to imagine that Andrew Morton has made such a mistake and that it may have gone uncorrected into his new book *William and Catherine:Their Lives, Their Wedding;* or is this the work of well-meaning sub-editing of the copy in Australia*, which I understand is now the practice? I think we should know.

*See page 194.

The Times **Turkeys for Christmas** 4 May

Sir, I have just been onto the National Trust's My Farm website ("A real Farmville will help us know our onions", Opinion, May 4) to find out more about the decisions that will be made by subscribers' regular votes and was relieved to find nothing about AV.

DTel   **Clear winner came**   7 May
                     first past the post

SIR - The Yes campaign was not defeated mainly because of the incoherence of the arguments (Letters, May 7) - they were perfectly clear. They lost because those voting No came first past the post and with an overwhelming majority.

The Times   9 May

Electoral reform and the future of the UK

Sir, Matthew Parris is disillusioned if he thinks it likely that, on Friday's results, asking voters to have ranked status quo, AV or proportional representation (PR) in order of preference would have produced a convincing win for AV (Opinion, May 7). Quite why any of the 69% who voted "No" would wish to rank either AV or PR first is a mystery and an assumption too far.

Faced with an order of preference, it is difficult to imagine "No" voters bothering to rank the other two at all; the second

preferences of the remaining 31% would have made no difference to the result. What commentators do not seem to understand, or accept, is that a "No" vote was not a vote against AV, but a vote for the status quo.

DTel **Claim to fame** 10 May

SIR - Michael Deacon invites readers to beat his claim to fame (Comment, Notebook, May 10). How about those who have danced with a girl, who's danced with a man, who's danced with the Duchess of Cambridge?

DTel **Personal gain** 11 May

SIR - Why do people have such difficulty with the English language? If David Laws has wrongly used tens of thousands of pounds of taxpayers' money to hide his sexuality, he has done so for personal gain because he has not had to use his own money to do so (News, May 11).

THE WIT AND WISDOM OF AN ORDINARY SUBJECT

The Times **Mincemeat giveaway** 22 May

Sir, The detail of the hoax in Ben Macintyre's BBC Two story of Operation Mincemeat was indeed gripping (Saturday Review, May 21). It was a good job that the documents on the corpse didn't depict the fictional officer, as in the programme, holding a cigarette between his thumb and middle finger. What a giveaway.

The Times **Good points** 11 Jun

Sir, I wonder what other motoring offences there are whereby points are deducted from a culprit's driving licence (letter, June 11). I am sure that they will be of particular interest to anyone who already has nine points on their licence.

The Times 18 Jun

Ascot apparel is far from ripping

Sir, What about buttoned-down shirt collars with a morning suit? Dreadful.

DTel **Volunteering not enough** 19 Jun

SIR - Officers and soldiers in the Army are not volunteering for voluntary redundancy (Report, June 18); they are volunteering to be considered for compulsory redundancy. As such, some of those who volunteer will not be made redundant and some of those who did not volunteer will be. Those retained because of their present and perceived future value to the Army can always apply to leave it after due notice, but they won't get any redundancy payments.

Daily Telegraph 24 Jun

Jumping up and down with frustration over fortnightly bin collection

SIR - Our council also recognises that packaging takes up at least half of domestic rubbish (Letters, June 24), but provides separate receptacles for bottles as well as for cardboard and plastic.

Our rubbish bin for the remainder varies from half-filled to full and is collected weekly; it is the separated bulked items that are collected every two weeks along with green waste.

This hygienic formula for collections within West Berkshire, with its mixture of rural and urban areas, works well.

DTel   **Modern Wimbledon**   25 Jun

SIR - Common courtesy seems to have gone from the handshake too (Letter, June 25), both sexes grasping hands upwards with their forearms at right-angles. And how long has a "passing shot" been returnable? That really would be a "big" shot (Last night on television, June 24).

The Times   **Care for the elderly**   30 Jun

Sir, A "once in a lifetime" chance to change something as important as care for the elderly is not the same as "the case for change could not be more compelling" (report, June 30). Emotive wording may make good sound bites, but should not be allowed to influence proper consideration of a government-commissioned review before it has even been published.

Such an important concern, for all those living and, on their behalf, their descendants deserves the best analysis of all the facts available, conceivable future scenarios and current best practice throughout the world, before timely decisions are taken on behalf of us all.

I look forward to reading the next attempt at this when the Andrew Dilnot's review is published on Monday.

The Times **Expenses not for profit** 15 Jul

Sir, David Aaronovitch states that the expenses scandal has led to an absurdly bureaucratic and complicated system of monitoring MPs' claims (Opinion, July 14). The scandal is that some MPs still seem to expect that they alone amongst both government and private sector employees should not have to produce receipts for valid claims. Add to that that some still dispute what is and is not valid and the system defines itself. The point about expenses is that they confer no financial benefit and as long as that is resented in some quarters, the bureaucracy and complication in the monitoring system will need to remain.

The Times **Boarders** 30 Jun

Sir, Those who did go to boarding school may also have noticed that there was something actually quite peculiar in some ways about those who didn't, but wouldn't have dreamt of writing about it, until now (letter, June 30). But let's face it, we all need each other.

DTel **Care costs and inflation** 5 Jul

SIR - The £35,000 cap on care costs, the cap for accommodation costs in residential care homes of between £7000 and £10,000, and the raising of the means-tested assets threshold to £100,000 are only the start of it. What safeguards will there be that these amounts will not be eroded by inflation, as with inheritance tax thresholds, before they are agreed and implemented, which is not expected to be until after the next general election, never mind when they are in place?

The Times **Care and inheritance** 6 Jul

Sir, Daniel Finkelstein is quite right. Mr Dilnot's solution is about inheritance (Opinion, July 6). Be it the £35,000 cap on care costs, the cap for accommodation costs in residential care homes of between £7000 and £10,000, or the raising of the means-tested assets threshold to £100,000, potential beneficiaries will be better off. But like inheritance tax thresholds, the caps are likely to be eroded by inflation. They will need to be decoupled from inheritance tax thresholds lest they are seen as an extension of inheritance tax, which will inevitably leave the 2009 freeze on the inheritance tax threshold to continue as part of the solution to costs.

2011

DTel **Downton Abbey blunders revisited** 8 Jul

SIR - A quick check on the internet reveals that two blue-eyed parents can have a brown-eyed child (Letters, July 8). According to geneticist Dr Barry Starr of Stanford University, genetics taught at GCSE is too simple to explain everything; genes can and do change from generation to generation (and even within the same person) producing this exception to the rule.

For me, an equally unlikely occurrence to register as a blunder is the hunting scene, also used in the DVD trailer, where Lady Mary, riding at a canter, turns to talk to the handsome visiting Turkish diplomat, Mr Kemal Pamuk, coming up alongside at a trot.

The Times **Rebekah Brooks** 8 Jul

Sir, The words of Rebekah Brooks's address to the staff of the *News of The World* have reminded me of that newspaper's role in the Profomo scandal of nearly 50 years ago, though not for its triumph, but for John Profumo's contrition. Actress Valerie Hobson supported her husband's dedication to the East End of London charity Toynbe Hall for the rest of his life, leading to his public recognition with the award of the CBE which signalled his return to respectability.

THE WIT AND WISDOM OF AN ORDINARY SUBJECT

DTel   **Bradman v Tendulkar**   12 Jul

SIR - Sir Donald Bradman is regarded as the greatest batsman of them all, although some think Tendulkar might have a claim (Sport, July 12). Though that claim will surely only be truly realised if *Tendulkaresque* enters cricket's lexicon.

The Times   **Online feedback in print**   16 Jul

Sir, You recently published a couple of letters whose contributors' addresses were attributed to *Online*. On Saturday (Opinion, July 16), Sally Baker's Feedback column quoted 10 further *Online* contributions. If this is the new way of getting grammatically expressed and otherwise printable views onto the printed page, then those sending their letters by e-mail could increase the chances of their views being published by pasting the content into the *Times Online* applications. In addition to the Letters to the Editor page, perhaps we can now look forward to a daily feedback page.

Dear Mr Watson,   21 Jul

Letters has passed this to me and I'll try to explain. The letters editor currently receives about 600 e-mailed and posted contributions daily, usually more than enough to choose from, so he does not routinely trawl through responses posted online looking for more. However, occasionally a colleague might draw his attention to something particularly interesting or valuable among the many online comments. My Feedback column, on the other hand, is a forum for readers' comments sent not only to myself but to any area of the paper, including online, so while I give priority to readers who contact me directly at Feedback, the Editor likes me whenever possible to trawl through comments posted online for interesting material to bring to a wider audience.

Sally Baker
Feedback editor, The Times

Private Eye **Commentatorballs** 17 Jul

"Even if it hadn't gone in, it was a wonderful touch."
MAUREEN MACKILL, The Open Championship, BBC1

The Times **Dress in the pavilion at Lord's** 22 Jul

Sir, I can assure Wendy Levis that there is no requirement to dress up to go into the cricket pavilion at Lord's (letter, July 22). It is dressing down that is frowned upon.

THE WIT AND WISDOM OF AN ORDINARY SUBJECT

DTel **Olympics hideaway** 28 Jul

SIR - Joan Bakewell wonders where to hide to avoid the cacophony of the forthcoming Olympics (Comment, July 28). I, for one, shall be pinning my hopes on some bargain offers this time next year to visit a part of the British Isles far from London, which I might not otherwise have thought of going to. I shall want mobile phone coverage and Sky TV for the cricket. Any suggestions?

The Times **Hawk-eye accuracy** 1 Aug

Sir, Vijay Lee is wrong when he says that the bounce shown by Hawk-Eye of a ball that hits the pads is guesswork (letter, August 1). It is a highly accurate prediction based on long established and well understood mathematics and physics. An acknowledged margin of error is already taken into account by the Decision Review System (DRS), which allows an umpire's Not Out decision to stand even though the ball may, on occasion, be shown to be clipping the wicket. India must adopt the DRS as soon as the current series is over, not least to be able to influence its future refinement, but also to benefit from its undoubted contribution to the increasing number of correct LBW decisions now being made.

DTel	**Peeling quails eggs**	2 Aug

SIR - The tiresome task of peeling boiled quails eggs (Letters, August 2) is best achieved by putting them into cold water and then peeling straight away. Keep a separate bowl of water at hand to rinse off any small pieces of egg shell remaining.
Jane Watson

DTel	**Riots - lessons learned**	10 Aug

SIR - Let's hear less from the police about lessons learned and more about lessons identified, as some of them might quite well have been learnt before, but forgotten.

The Times	**No 1 Test team**	13 Aug

Sir, I have followed every England Test match since 1961 and my abiding interest has never wavered, however well or badly the England team has done. I have nothing but admiration for the achievements of the present England side and the way they have gone about their rise to be the No 1 Test match team in the world. But I wonder if I am alone in finding that there is now nothing to talk about with fellow England supporters, or critics, apart from who plays if one of the team is injured - no debate about the balance of the side, who the selectors are, or which players or counties they favour; no captaincy debate, or team governance issues.

We have even got used to the strip they wear and, as cable-stitch pullovers are no longer worn, the sun seems to shine more often when they play. Long may it do so, but staying at the top will be another matter, when the debates will resume; but in the meantime, congratulations are due to all concerned.

The Oldie   **Call it a book review?**   13 Aug
                       Not in my day, Sir!

SIR: In spite of being given out LBW by one of the correspondents in *Not in My Day, Sir: Cricket Letters to The Daily Telegraph, edited by Martin Smit*h, Robert Low does not seem to have sufficient knowledge of cricket to write a credible review of this wonderful collection of letters (Books, August *Oldie*).

Certainly the letter he envisaged sending to the editor of the book to complain "about the lack of introductory information about the major issues under consideration" would not have caused any alarm, because they are all clearly mentioned in the carefully crafted Introduction to the book, with many repeated on the flap of the dust jacket.

So it's not surprising then, I suppose, that an unheard of term such as "declaring batsmen out" replaces a correspondent's "forcing them to retire". Or that Lord Fisher's letter in 1968 is said to be about Basil d'Oliveira not being selected to tour South

Africa in 1970, when the tour was to have taken place in 1968/69. The South Africans were due to come over here in 1970 for a tour, until that too was cancelled.

No wonder retired colonels everywhere continue to write to all sorts of publications, particularly about cricket, if this is all the accuracy we can expect from reviewers of our efforts.

Colonel (retd) J M C Watson

| *STel* | **Social order and stability or defence of the realm** | 4 Aug |

SIR - Maintaining social order and stability is the primary function of government (Leading article, August 14). But it is also said that the first and overwhelming duty of any government is the defence of the realm. The first is carried out by the police and the second by the armed forces. The time has now come for the priority between function and duty to be reconciled with a coherent and comprehensive policy for the full and graduated use of all the forces of the Crown to fulfil the cogent aim of keeping us safe.

| *DTel /The Times* | **Novel job-share** | 19/27 Aug |

SIR - How interesting to read of the appointments of Mr Jonathan James Aves and Ms Katherine Jane Leach as a husband-and-wife team to be Her Majesty's Joint Ambassadors to Armenia (Register,

August 17), presumably for a single salary to cover their four-monthly rotation. How extraordinary, though, that they should not wish to represent Her Majesty and present themselves as Mr and Mrs Aves.

DTel **Army and RAF redundancies** 1 Sep

SIR - Your political correspondent makes the often made mistake of differentiating between voluntary and compulsory redundancies being announced for members of the Army and the RAF (Report, September 1). They are all being made compulsorily redundant, though some of them have volunteered to be made so.

This is to safeguard their redundancy payments from additional tax. Payments made to those resigning voluntarily are generally seen as a 'golden handshake' or terminal bonus and, as such, subject to the normal tax and National Insurance Contribution rules. By using a compulsory redundancy scheme, MOD ensures that payments up to £30,000 are tax free for all those made redundant, whether they have volunteered or not.

DTel **Sneak previews** 2 Sep

SIR - A quick sneak on the internet reveals a "sort of" preview as an appropriate teaser (Letters, Sept 2); and there is a preview of the Queen's 2008 Christmas message, about which there can be nothing sneaky at all.

The Times **Learning with Radio** 2 Sep

Sir, I expect that not everyone listening to Radio 3, or reading *The Times*, will necessarily know that a movement of a work does not stand on its own (letter, Sept 2). Perhaps these morning schedules have an educational part to play as well, without further alienating the discerning listener later in the day.

The Times **Armed forces redundancies** 2 Sep

Sir, Some of the Army's highest ranking officers have not applied for voluntary redundancy ("Army on alert as talented officers ask for a payoff", Sept 2). Commodore Woodcock, Head of Armed Forces and Manning, comments more accurately that "some long-serving senior officers are applying to be made redundant".

The fact is that they are all being made compulsorily redundant, though some of them have volunteered to be made so. This is principally to safeguard their redundancy payments from additional tax. A payments made to those resigning voluntarily is generally seen as a 'golden handshake' or terminal bonus and, as such, subject to the normal tax and National Insurance Contribution rules. By using a compulsory redundancy scheme, MOD can retain the talent it wants and ensure that payments, currently up to £30,000, are tax free for all those made redundant.

Those retained for their particular talents can always apply to leave the Army after due notice, but they won't get any redundancy payments. The real alert will sound if many of them choose to do so.

DTel   **Autumn colours**   10 Sep

SIR - Your advertisement for Booster Cushions at Unbeatable Prices (Weekend, September 10) shows a picture of red, green and brown cushions. Their designated colours? Terracotta, fern and mink.

DTel   **Fuel economy in cars**   12 Sep

SIR - The return journey by car from Pollington to The Deep in Hull would have involved 73 miles of mixed motorway, rural and urban driving (Letters, September 12). According to Fuel-Economy.co.uk, the most efficient petrol car which can take 4 passengers has a combined miles per gallon (MPG) of 51.50; for diesel it is 68.90. With petrol now costing £6 a gallon and diesel even more, I think we should know which remarkable car and driving technique would have been used to complete this journey for less than £5. If it is the petrol hybrid Honda Insight with a combined MPG of 83.10, then perhaps the price tag of £16,995 would also need to be taken into consideration.

DTel   **Welcome back Downton Abbey**   18 Sep

SIR - They're all there, the trappings of military service: epaulettes, belt buckles, polished cap straps, but too often not in the right place, or the same one from shot to shot. (And that was before the bullet that took out the medic below the line of the parapet).

The Times   17 Sep

Hoops and hurdles

Sir, Whether designs for private houses and extensions submitted by qualified architects conform to general principles or not (letter, Sept 16), one man's architectural merit is another man's carbuncle.

Whatever the "hoops", some "hurdles" should remain.

Times Feedback   **Accuracy and analysis**   18 Sep

Madam , Victoria Hislop states ("Must this be a Greek tragedy?", times 2, Sept 16) that "Deaths on the road in Crete last summer were at least 400 per cent higher than in UK. There is no need for analysis on this." Well, I'm afraid there is.

Data is hard to find on "summers", but for full years it appears that both UK and Greece had under 2000 road deaths in 2010. Within Greece, Crete had the worst regional figure with 89 - hardly 4 times more than UK. What I suspect Hislop intended was to compare rates per million of population. For UK that was 69 and for Greece 130, still only just under twice UK's rate. However, the population of Crete is only 650,000, which gives 137 per million - now up to double UK's rate. Allowing for summer variations in Crete may send the rate up, but doubling it again to 4 times? I should like to see the statistically significant evidence.

Hislop goes on: "Similarly, smoking is still a popular pastime…" and "This self-destructive tendency seems to be quite deep-rooted." Had she found the life expectancy on Crete less than in the UK, which it isn't, no doubt she would have been telling them all to cover up more before going out in the sun. Thank goodness for some diversity between nations.

2011

DTel /*Times*   **Faster than Einstein**   23/26 Sep

Sir, During a university lecture nearly 40 years ago now, a professor used the questionable equation $c^2 = xy$, where c was the speed of light ("An idiot's guide to the special theory of relativity", News, Science, Sept 24). As either x or y would have been greater than c, perhaps he was well ahead of his time.

DTel   **Guyabera shirts**   29 Sep

SIR - With the arrival of the Indian summer, I have just got out a *guyabera* shirt from my time overseas for this weekend's barbecue. Worn widely in Central America and Cuba, and coming with short or long sleeves, these are the ultimate for pocket space.

As well as 2 breast pockets, they have 2 deep frontal ones at hip-level. Not only is there room for glasses and a bus pass (Letters, September 29), they can carry my mobile phone, diary, wallet, and, yes, cigar case, cutter and lighter for outdoor use.

The Times   **Wrong side down under**   29 Sep

Sir, As the monarch of Niue, the Queen's head is not on the reverse side of their special commemorative coins, but the obverse (News, Sept 29). It is the Star Wars' characters that are on the reverse.

The Oldie   **Armistice Day 2111**   30 Sep

SIR: I feel that John Glenister may be confused about Armistice Day (Readers Write, October *Oldie*). A palindromic date in the form 11.11.11 appears not just this year, but each century. Of course, in the 20th century the First World War had not started. Whether Armistice Day will still be commemorated in 2111 is another matter. However, as there are now no national commemorations of conflicts fought before 1914, I would suspect not, but "never again" is conjecture.

The Guardian   3 Oct

Navy redundancies

It is not correct to say that one third of 1,100 Royal Navy redundancies will be compulsory - they all will (Report, 30 September). The MoD runs a compulsory redundancy scheme, for which two-thirds have volunteered. This is principally to safeguard their redundancy payments from additional tax.

2011

The Week   **MoD redundancies**   8 Oct

To The Guardian

"The MoD runs a compulsory redundancy scheme, for which two-thirds have volunteered" Is this an example of "military intelligence"?
Root Cartwright, Radlett, Hertfordshire

The Times   **UK speed limits**   5 Oct

Sir, Has anyone seen any of the "white" goods vans limited to 60 mph on motorways and 50 mph on dual carriageways actually stick to these limits, or does one have to have attended a speed awareness course to have heard of them?

Sunday Times   **Whose honour now?**   5 Oct

Advancing armies try to capture bridges intact; withdrawing armies blow them up to try and prevent them from doing so. The Japanese did not blow up the causeway linking Singapore to the Malayan mainland, as claimed by Dominic Sandbrook in his review of Sir Max Hastings' new book, *All Hell Let Loose* (Culture, October 2, page 43), the British did. Nor did the author say the Japanese had done so either.

In trying to spark interest by starting his review with the story of Lee Kuan Yew from page 211, the reviewer has let himself and the author down by not picking up the clue from the next sentence: "For fifty-five days, the Japanese had maintained a daily average advance of twelve miles, fighting ninety-five engagements and repairing 250 bridges." To adopt the words of Churchill's signal concerning the British Empire and the British Army, perhaps it is the honour of the author and the reviewer that are at stake now.
Col J M C Watson (retd)

DTel **Gents' for ladies** 11 Oct

SIR - Our warm and generous hosts this weekend proudly announced during the ensuing levity that the petite lady of the house avoided queues at public lavatories by using the gentlemen's (Letters, October 10). Apparently, the men wonder if they are in the right place; and a quick exit without eye contact, personal or in the mirror, avoids any adverse reaction and minimises the length of time involved (Letters, October 11).

The Times **Lack of moral courage** 18 Oct
in the NHS

Sir, Roger Hayes has confirmed from his personal knowledge, what many of us have witnessed from our own experiences, that the fundamental problem with the performance of the NHS is lack of leadership and managerial effectiveness (letter, Oct 15). "The leadership to know and show what should be done, and management to see that it is done, providing training and discipline as necessary" could not put it more clearly or succinctly. But nothing will happen until those chairs and chief executives of trust boards that he identifies as responsible summon up the moral courage to act. It may only take one or two of them to set the ball rolling, but if they don't, to coin a phrase, the worst offenders should have their positions considered for them.

DTel **What is an Australian?** 19 Oct

SIR - Oscar Humphries asks (Comment, October 19) "what is an Australian?" To adapt what I once heard a Canadian comedian say about his fellow countrymen: an Australian is an immigrant with seniority.

The Times 24 Oct

Pulling teeth

Sir, Lord Howe, the Health Minister, says that no one should be left without access to a GP (letter, Oct 21). I wonder when he will be able to say the same about access to NHS dentists.

The Times   **United by a common language**   25 Oct

Sir, Does anyone seriously think that the United States of America or the Estados Unidos de México would have come to fruition if their states had spoken different languages? Ultimately, Europe is going to fail not only because there isn't a common language (letter, Oct 25), but because there will never be one.

Daily Telegraph   29 Oct

Downton Abbey

SIR - Norman Dodd (Letters, October 29) wonders why Lord Grantham is in uniform but never leaves the house. He is obviously trying to leave, since he has put his Sam Browne belt on (Letter, October 26). But his belt buckle is never in the right position, making him "improperly dressed" and so not allowed out.

STel	**Bathtime**	30 Oct

SIR - Philip Styles' letter (October 30) about taking his monthly bath reminded me of two favourite one-liners. When asked if he'd taken a bath, the actor Tony Curtis replied: "No, why? Is there one missing?" And when Eric Morecambe announced that he was going to have one, Ernie Wise's riposte was: "It's not October already is it?"

DTel	**Sloe gin slip-up**	31 Oct

SIR - Last year, I accidently mixed a jar of sloe gin with four times as much damson gin, which I was making at the same time. The result: "damsloe" gin, and damned good it is too.

    Also, save the gin soaked damsons in a jar and have them with crème fraîche - delicious.

The Cricketer	Nov issue

Never ending tour

Think the Indians suffered in England this summer. Try telling the 1959 tourists. After the Oval Test, which sealed their 5-0 defeat, the Indian players had five more first-class matches to play, finally finishing with a 2-day match against Durham at Sunderland. Their 37-match tour ended a fully three weeks after their defeat at The Oval.

DTel	**Primary error**	3 Nov

SIR - Primary colours may lack a certain humanity, but green is not one of them (Leading Article, November 3). How apt then that the car park commemorating Nurse Cavell in Peterborough has been renamed Green, for which one primary colour "is not enough". I suppose we must be thankful that it isn't Yellow.

DTel/The Times	**Pronunciation of**	5/18 Nov
The Oldie	**the word "protest"**	17 Nov

SIR - One aspect of the situation outside St Paul's Cathedral, which doesn't seem to have been commented on so far, is the frequent inability of some newsreaders and reporters, on both television and radio, to differentiate between the pronunciation of the word *protest* when spoken as a verb or a noun, and to pronounce properly *protesting* and *protesters*.

Other languages, such as Spanish, cater in part for such differences by using accents on individual letters. Those taught English well as a foreign language, and Americans, seem to get it right more regularly (Letter, November 5).

Has the time come for some form of emphasis to be introduced to autocues and scripts used in the broadcast media and some training for those not using either?

Private Eye **Pseuds Corner** 5 Nov

"Where one painting might make anyone marvel, his works together weave an ever-more intricate web. You can grasp hold of the threads. But it's the untouchable spaces between them that create the fragile miracle."
From RACHEL CAMPBELL-JOHNSTON's review of the Leonardo da Vinci exhibition at the National Gallery in *The Times*.

The Times **Interruptions to the *Today* programme** 5 Nov

Sir, When will the presenters on the BBC Radio 4 *Today* programme begin to understand that the swiftness of their interruptions, of Cabinet ministers in particular, is too often inversely proportional to their credibility as interviewers and increases the validity of interviewees' responses? Sarah Montagues's interview of the Chancellor of the Exchequer on Friday was a classic example.

THE WIT AND WISDOM OF AN ORDINARY SUBJECT

The Times   **Over the top**   12 Nov

Sir, If the fine imposed on Mike Tindall was not "over the top", then, quite simply, his remuneration has to have been.

DTel   **Champagne is never cheap**   15 Nov

SIR - There is nothing "cheap" about champagne, wherever it is bought (News, November 15). But how refreshing to hear of four "low cost" supermarket brands that eclipsed the luxury versions of some well known champagne houses in a blind tasting.

Champagne has always been overpriced, apparently at levels that the predominantly British market will stand. It would be interesting to know which houses contributed to the winners in these more austere times.

Evening Standard   18 Nov

Smoking in cars

Far too many drivers get away with using hand-held phones in cars as the law is unenforceable. It would be the same for a ban on smoking. **J M C Watson**

Daily Telegraph 21 Nov

Mellifluous tones

SIR - May I add to the list of wonderful female voices on the radio those of Fran Godfrey and Fenella Fudge from Radio 2. Their clarity does wonders for the Queen's English.

DTel **Correct form at the Palace** 23 Nov

SIR - Why is it now Vice Admiral Sir Tim Lawrence, but Sir Augustine O'Donnell (Court Circular, November 23)? Sir Timothy, surely?

The Times/D Tel **Winter fuel payments** 24/29 Nov

Sir, My wife has been informed by letter from the Pension Service that her mother, for whom she has power of attorney, is to receive a £150 winter fuel payment. The service was informed at the time, that she had gone into a care home on 26th May 2010. Since 1st November 2010, her needs there have been fully funded under the NHS Continuing Healthcare (CHC) provision. Naturally this includes heating. Last year, it transpires that she was credited with a £400 payment on 30th November.

On ringing the Pension Service, it was explained that she was entitled to both of these payments under the rules. When questioned about the sense of one government department paying out for what was already being paid for by another, I was told that the fuel entitlements were legislative decisions, but the money did not have to be spent on fuel. No one was prepared to record this anomaly and report it upwards.

On receipt of CHC funding, as is required, my wife wrote to the Disability and Carers Service, whereupon her mother's entitlement to Attendance Allowance of £285 every four weeks rightly ceased. Both these services come under the same Department of Work and Pensions and what is required of the beneficiary for one can surely be adapted for use by the other. If there isn't an awards' scheme in the department(s) to incentivise the identification of such savings and unwarranted expenditure, then there certainly should be. If there is one, then it appears it may not be known about widely enough.

Failing that, I do hope that the calls were indeed recorded and will be used for more than just "training purposes".

DTel	**Most important jobs**	1 Dec

SIR - Understandably, Dr Sheldon, the Master of Wellington College, and his Common Room contend that there is no more important job than educating our young (Letters, 1 December). They may well be right, but there are other contenders for such an accolade. Top amongst those who might be paid for their work would be farmers and doctors; and amongst those who may not be, parents and carers, jobs which can also be amongst the most difficult.

DTel	**High Street Duke**	7 Dec

SIR - Does the Duchess of Cambridge's wearing of outfits which button up like the Duke's (High Street Duchess, December 7) offer discrete support for those urging an end to male primogeniture?

DTel	**Examinations - little content**	9 Dec

SIR - In answer to a Sixties' "O" Level Chemistry question "Name a non-electrolyte", a fellow pupil said he had written down "A leg of mutton". It wasn't quite the answer the examination board had been looking for. But today, it looks as if it might be worth another try.

THE WIT AND WISDOM OF AN ORDINARY SUBJECT

DTel **Revitalisation of town centres** 14 Dec

SIR - May I commend Ryde, on the Isle of Wight, as an example of town centre revitalisation (Letters, December 14). Once rather run-down, it is now full of interesting independent shops. Free parking on the streets helps shoppers, and the various cafes, pubs and restaurants in amongst them seem to be flourishing, even in December. Major factors appear to have been the arrival in the town of a small supermarket, with free parking space, to counteract the out-of-town giant and the introduction of the small business rate relief 3 years ago. A further extension of the relief beyond April next year can only be of continued benefit to town centres nationwide.

The Times **Unreal private sector jobs** 14 Dec

Sir, There are known unfilled real jobs; these are jobs that we know the unemployed do not want to do. We also know there are non-jobs in the public sector; that is to say jobs that we know must go and will not be replaced there by real jobs. But there are also unreal jobs – these are jobs that the private sector is expected to create even when we know they have no real need.

(With apologies to Donald Rumsfeld, US Secretary of Defense, 12th February 2002.)

Times Feedback **Double exposure** 22 Dec

Madam , Alongside John Keast's letter (Dec 22) on religious education is the notice "Letters should ... be exclusive to *The Times*."; your response to email submissions states that letters *must* be exclusive to *The Times*. And yet *The Daily Telegraph* has published with equal prominence on the same day the same letter from him with minor editorial changes.

I wonder if my restraint (and success) in only writing to the other if not published in the first is misguided, or are some subjects more worthy than others? Some guidance please.

Dear Mr Watson,   *23 Dec*

We tell readers clearly – on the page and in the automatic acknowledgment of emails – that their letters should be exclusive. The Telegraph policy, stated or not, is the same. The odd correspondent chooses to take no notice, with the results you observe. I don't imagine it makes much difference to anyone apart from a small number of particularly keen devotees of newspaper correspondence columns; most readers take just one paper and don't care in the least about the others. But I can assure you that we – and the letters team at the Telegraph - find it intensely annoying, and that we are likely to look much less kindly on future offerings from the correspondents concerned.
Yours sincerely, Ian Brunskill
Editor, Letters, Obituaries & Register, The Times

The Times **Mr Clegg and clichés** 23 Dec

Sir, As one of the great cliché mongers of contemporary politics ("Lawmakers needed: experience essential", Dec23), Mr Clegg should "beware what he wishes" with the House of Lords, as "politics is the art of the possible" and "all political careers end in failure."

Daily Telegraph 29 Dec

Red wine with lobster

SIR - It is not only experts who say that, sometimes, one kind of wine should be drunk with foods traditionally associated with another kind ("Want a wine ripe for the cheese platter? Stay with the red", report, December 26).

I once dined next to a friend who had recently returned after two years in France. The occasion was a black-tie dinner at which lobster was served as the main course. When it arrived, however, my friend continued to drink her red from the first course.

I enquired tentatively why she had turned down the white now being offered with the lobster. "Oh," she replied, "one never drinks the white unless one knows the grower."

DTel **Smarter teachers** 30 Dec

SIR- Whatever happened to pride in appearance?

2012

Sunday Telegraph   1 Jan

Random allocation of Silver Jubilee Medal

SIR - The 1977 Queen's Silver Jubilee Medal was also a bone of contention among those serving. Most regiments received only seven, to be allocated at the commanding officer's discretion. Some regarded it as so contentious that they held a lottery.

DTel   **Diamond Jubilee stamps –**   2 Jan
                      the full picture

SIR - It is not correct that the Queen's Diamond Jubilee will be commemorated by a series of special stamps depicting the last five British monarchs (In Brief, January 2). This refers to the House of Windsor set, to be issued on February 2, completing the Kings & Queens series.

On February 6, to mark the 60th anniversary of the Queen's accession to the throne, a new 1st class Machin definitive is to be issued in a new "diamond blue" colour.

The set of commemorative stamps to mark the Queen's Diamond Jubilee, with designs that have yet to be announced, will be issued on May 31, making a fitting start to the Diamond Jubilee Weekend.

The Times **Lutyens and swimming pools** 3 Jan

Sir, It is not the British Embassy in Washington which is part of Sir Edwin Lutyens' legacy, but the Ambassador's Residence (Leading Article, Jan 3). Mr Boucherayer-Mallet dreads the thought of a swimming pool ever being put into the garden of his Lutyens' mock Tudor manor, Le Bois de Moutiers, near Dieppe ("Threat to corner of a foreign field that is forever England", Jan 3). In a reversal of fortune, a small new 'secret' garden has recently been added below the swimming pool area at the residence in Washington.

DTel **Testing times** 4 Jan

SIR - Professor Waters' comment that examinations are ruining school for children (report, January 4) reminded me of a military parachute course I undertook when an officer cadet. Completing our seven jumps whilst billeted in the comparative luxury of the officers' mess at RAF Abingdon, a fellow cadet remarked on leaving that it wouldn't have been a bad course if it hadn't been for the parachuting.

DTel **War Horse must run on** 17 Jan

SIR - I do hope that Charles Moore has not stolen the thunder of any potential letter writers, preventing a new and enjoyable trail, with his Downtonesque critique of Steven Spielburg's film *War Horse* (Comment, January 16). The lack of characterisation may be unforgiveable, but so would leaving unpublished other readers' observations.

DTel **Joan Bakewell – no tart there** 19 Jan

SIR - I venture to suggest that Joan Bakewell does not have an accent (News, January 19). She merely speaks the words as they are supposed to be spoken.

DTel **Don't bet on backgammon harmony** 20 Jan

SIR - Backgammon is a game for gambling which uses a doubling dice for players to raise their agreed starting stake during a game. A player's perceived chance of winning can be backed by doubling the current stake - in turn - after the first offer is made and accepted. Games end and the stake is lost, when its doubling is not accepted.

Thus the true measure of skill between players is the difference in treasure played for, or £3m as alluded to by Peter Watson and not the 4 games in over 22,000 played by Michael Brotherton (Letters,

January 20). The secret of maintaining marital harmony, though, is almost certainly leaving the doubling dice in the box.

DTel **Ties for security** 21 Jan

SIR - I am the proud owner of over 100 ties and, during a day at the races, I admired the tie being worn by a security guard at Ascot (Letters, January 20 and 21). Meeting up at the end of the day, he offered me his. A quick tug on the blade released a clip-on tie with the ready-tied knot. "Health and safety" he said, but it didn't join my collection.

The Times **Flight of fantasy** 23 Jan

Sir, So England's top scorer in the first Test match in Dubai, Matt Prior, thinks that, in defiance of the laws of physics, "the ball comes down slower" on Asian wickets ("Prior raring to go after 'a smack in the face' from Ajmal", Sport, Jan 23). Presumably the rest thought they were playing on the moon. Let's hope they come down to earth for the second Test in Abu Dhabi.

THE WIT AND WISDOM OF AN ORDINARY SUBJECT

The Times **Not united, but still great** 28 Jan

Sir, The names suggested by John Purvis for our country without Scotland (letter, Jan 28) smack too much of Little Britain for me. If we couldn't be united, let us at least put ourselves forward as something great. As a Yorkshireman, I personally would go for Yorkshire & The Rest.

STel **Yes and no for Scotland** 1 Feb

SIR - Robert Henderson says it is well established that humans are predisposed to agree and say yes, rather than disagree and say no and suggests that to avoid bias a neutral question would have two options with a box against each in a referendum on Scotland (Letters, January 29). It is also well established that humans are predisposed to be averse to change. The 69% no vote in last year's rejection of the alternative vote (AV) was actually a resounding yes for the status quo.

The ballot paper for the AV contained a statement ahead of a single (neutral) question. In a referendum question on Scotland, this precedent would transpose to: "At present, Scotland is part of the United Kingdom of Great Britain and Northern Ireland. Should Scotland be independent instead?" With the question neutralised, the second predisposition comes to the fore. When all the arguments, both for and against, have been debated and are fully understood by those entitled to vote and who do so, the most likely outcome must also be a no vote, resulting in another convincing yes for the status quo, whoever is enfranchised and whatever political commentators may have to say at the time.

The Oldie   Feb issue

Not many alive

SIR: Your readers may like to be updated about Donald Bradman's 1948 Australian touring team to England (Letter, *The Oldie*, December 2010). Sam Loxton died in December, aged 90. This leaves Arthur Morris, who will be 90 in January and Neil Harvey, only 19 when he toured, aged 83 as the last survivors.

Evening Standard   **Not practice – no ball**   1 Feb

The picture of Jimmy Anderson in the cricket nets in Dubai shows him bowling a no ball of spot-fixing proportions (Sport, 1 Feb). What sort of practice is that?
J M C Watson

The Times **King's funeral on the small screen** 7 Feb

Sir, Whilst readers older than myself will remember seeing in the cinema Pathé News of the events around the time of the King's death (letter, Feb 7), it was the coverage of the King's funeral that lingers as my first memory of television, having turned four just four days before his death.

DTel **An equally powerful predictor** 11 Feb

SIR - If, as David Halpern suggests (report, February 10), pensioners are less likely to be alive for more than a decade if they are lonely than if they smoke, then there would appear to be no incentive for them not to smoke for the good of their health.

Anyway, you were not supposed to feel alone with a cigarette called *Strand* and wasn't happiness a cigar called *Hamlet*? I would also like to suggest that some accompanying halves of *Top Totty* ale, if they can get hold of any (another report, February 10), would be an equally "powerful predictor" of a welcome lift to morale and relief from loneliness, however short-lived.

The Times	**Not so comic**	13 Feb

Sir, Whilst serving in the British Embassy in Washington in the late eighties as a lieutenant colonel, I made regular calls on a major general in the Pentagon. One day he pointed to a row of books in his office and said they were what I understood to be Beano albums (letter, 7 Feb). He then explained that they were congressional reports which demanded that "there will *be no* more of this".

The Times	**Pedestrian obstacles**	15 Feb

Sir, In your picture on the Letters page, (Cyclists in Edinburgh: raising awareness among drivers and cyclists is crucial, Feb 15), what on earth did the pedestrians think they were doing?

The Times		18 Feb

Return to duty

Sir, I wonder if there are any ex-Service personnel who do *not* use their service number on a briefcase combination lock.
MALCOLM WATSON
(Number withheld) Col (ret'd)

THE WIT AND WISDOM OF AN ORDINARY SUBJECT

DTel **Shot in the foot** 21 Feb

SIR - I would not dispute what David Taylor has to say about shooting on National Trust estates (Letter, February 20). However, as a member, I wonder what evidence he has, to say with such conviction, that its prevention is not "the wish of the Trust's paying members". Sadly, I suspect that it might well be.

STel **Civil Service efficiency** 22 Feb

SIR - I have just received a letter from HMRC which starts "We have not heard from you since our last letter. This may be because you have already notified us you have no liability to pay, in which case you do not need to take any further action." With no liability, I informed them immediately on receipt of the first letter. By not taking timely action on this information themselves, I can only imagine that there must be some performance-related pay involved in the number of letters that are sent out by HMRC, rather than in making savings on those that don't need to be.

Evening Standard **RBS bonuses and** 23 Feb
the man on the Clapham omnibus

By what measure understandable to the man on the Clapham omnibus, does RBS pay bonuses worth

£785 million after losses incurred have increased from £1.2 billion in 2010 to £2 billion last year; and what does he make of Stephen Hester's claim that the increased losses are evidence of "immense progress" in getting the bank back on track? (News, February 23). This is reward for failure on a grand scale and he can only wonder at how he can join in the failure, get onto this track and obtain some of the reward. After all, a halved bonus is better than none.

J M C Watson

DTel **Cheque's in the post** 25 Feb

SIR - I was pleased to read that the Oxford University Conservative Association had settled its bill from the Cavalry and Guards Club ("Oxford Tories who failed to play £12,000 bill", February 25). However, the club is in Piccadilly and not Pall Mall, where an equally dim view might have been taken of the guest of honour, Dr Liam Fox, wearing a suit at a black-tie banquet. This was disrespectful to his hosts, whoever they may be, or wherever they may have sent their cheque.

DTel **Broken cassette ribbon** 29 Feb

SIR - Not only do I have a car with a cassette player (Letter, February 29), but the ribbon on one of my favourite tapes is broken. Can I still get it spliced back together again?

The Times 2 Mar

Tear here

Sir, I am not sure that Mr Rogerson is right in inquiring about the "art" of perforation (letter, Mar 1), but the "science" surely rests with an industry that still produces lavatory paper which rarely tears along the perforations.

Daily Telegraph 12 Mar

Unusual pet names can be music to the ears

SIR – Max Craven (Letters, March 10) is concerned so many dogs are called Max. I took it as a great compliment when one of my sailors named his dog Watson, and he never kicked it in my sight.

Chris Watson
Carlton River, Tasmania, Australia

Daily Telegraph   14 Mar

A pet name that suggests one's in the doghouse

SIR - Our keeshond, or Dutch barge dog, is called Xochi (pronounced *zochi*) after Xochimilco, the colourful network of canals near Mexico City (Letters, March 12).

I am generally known as Watson, so I know that I am heading for a kicking if I hear my wife calling me "Malcolm".

SIR – My elder son also named his dog Watson.
John Holmes
Crookham Village, Hampshire

The Times   **Care home comforts for some**   15 Mar

Sir, Nick Sanderson, CEO, Audley Retirement Villages, is too sweeping in his assertion that: "No one, no matter their age, wants to live in a care home." (letter, Mar 15). "No one.....wants to be *sent to* live in a care home" would more accurately reflect reality. Some opt to live in a care home of their own volition and for a variety of reasons; to imply that they do not know their own minds is insensitive.

DTel **Reversing a damp squib** 27 Mar

SIR - Spotting gentlemen's evening shirts buttoned the correct way in one scene and then the opposite way in another indicates that the £11 million budget for ITV's most expensive drama ever, *Titanic*, did not run to the mirror image sets of clothing used in James Cameron's blockbuster film of 1997.

This technique requires only one side of the ship to be built as a set and provides authenticity to scenes on the other side when the film is projected in reverse. Without reversed items, we are in for some interesting "spotting" in the remaining episodes.

Times Feedback **My two penn'orth** 27 Mar

Madam, Since subscribing to *The Times* online a few weeks ago, I have taken to reading the paper in the order that various parts of it seem to be posted. To date this means reading the letters as early as 6.30pm the night before the paper is available and even seeing comments on them from New Jersey and further west, where they can in effect read tomorrow's paper today. On Fridays this even extends to Feedback.

The Times   **Last words**   27 Mar
from Jeremy Paxman

Sir, Jeremy Paxman says that your story about the HMRC and service companies is partly true (letter, Mar 26). I suggest that the words he ended his series, *Empire*, with on BBC 1 on Monday night: "it's time we stopped pretending the Empire was nothing to do with us", are not true at all.

The Times   **Cigar smoking etiquette**   28 Mar

Sir, A British gentleman, as depicted by Peter Brookes (Cartoon, Mar 28), would not be smoking a cigar with the band still on it, have folded his napkin, or not have the insteps of his soles blackened.

DTel   **Lessons still to be learned**   31 Mar

SIR - Before lessons can be learned, whether by the main political parties or in our heritage cities (Letters, March 31), they must first be identified and captured. A lesson that has been identified should lead to a recommendation; a lesson learned needs to be accompanied by an action.

The benefits come from ensuring that the lessons are actually applied, which is the difficult part, especially when previous decisions are called into question and may need to be overturned. This is the essence of a U turn, whether announced outside No 10 Downing Street or conducted in a car on a minor road.

DTel **Sausage roller** 3 Apr

SIR - Amongst over 100 free range products available from our nearest supermarket are "Free Range Pork & Onion Marmalade Sausages" and "Free Range Egg Noodles". I could go on…

The Times **Arms and the man** 5 Apr

Sir, Unfortunately, for all the pubs and pub names that are being lost (letters, Apr 4 and 5), a few of those remaining seem to be in danger of morphing into the "Grievous Bodily Arms", especially in our inner cities.

Country Life   4 Apr

No feud like an old feud

Your School Life supplement (March 14) rightly lists the sporting rivalry between Oundle and Uppingham amongst the best school feuds. But Phil Spencer's memory is letting him down if he thinks that Oundle were always trounced. The speedy bowling out of Uppingham on the cricket field in 1999, described by Will Jefferson, was exceptional and masks a more even balance of results down the generations. I note that the Uppingham 1st XV has not beaten Oundle on the rugby field since the same year. As it is said of other sporting encounters: "a good big 'un will always beat a good little 'un....".

J. M. C. Watson (Oundle 1961-66)

DTel   **Who are the masters now?**   9 Apr

SIR - Marvellous - a Watson is back. But Peter Allis must surely now bow out as a commentator. To describe Bubba Watson's amazing second shot on the final hole of the Masters' playoff as "a smash and hope for the best" was surely too out of touch for the modern era. At least, unlike in 2009, he realised there was to be a playoff. Step up Colin Montgomerie.

DTel   **Don't be chicken of**   11 Apr
                 language training

SIR - Whilst the defence attaché at our embassy in Mexico City, I arranged a briefing for European colleagues, early in my tour in 1998, from the ministry for the army and air force about the internal security situation in their southern state of Chiapas. After the briefing, which was conducted over coffee and biscuits, but without a map or any other visual aid, I commented to my French colleague that whatever else was happening, there seemed to be a lot of chickens (*pollo* in Spanish, pronounced *poyo*) running around down there. I had misunderstood the word *apoyo*, meaning support, which made much more sense.

Telling this story against myself in Havana, where I was also accredited, did much more to endear me to my Cuban minders than the greater fluency of my fellow attachés, though I remain full of admiration for the ambassadors whom I served and other senior staff, whose level of language ability was every bit as high as that recalled as necessary by Charles Crawford (Comment, April 11); and it showed and mattered.

Private Eye   **Commentatorballs**   7 Apr

"The man out in the deep will cut off a certain boundary."
MICHAEL ATHERTON, Sky Sports 1

The Times   11 Apr

Regulation lottery

Sir, The four peers appealing about the National Lottery being undermined by the Health Lottery may be too late (letter, Apr 5). No sooner had I read that "the longer the period of regulatory inaction, the more incentive there is for other organisations to set up similar rival lotteries", than details of two such enterprises came through the letterbox. The Royal British Legion's Poppy Lottery and a lottery for The Children's Trust, together with the Health Lottery, are all offering nationwide weekly prizes for a starting stake of £1.

Raising funds has always depended on the energy and ingenuity of the charities concerned and these latest lotteries with their offer a greater chance of winning smaller, but still significant amounts of money, may well appeal to those who do not buy National Lottery tickets. They deserve our support and it will be a travesty if the costs of setting them up, let alone future ticket sales, are now to be lost through untimely regulatory or political action.

DTel **Shocked Aussie overheard** 17 Apr

SIR - After a performance of *"Les Patterson has a Stand-Up"* at the Whitehall Theatre, in which Barry Humphries played the Australian Cultural Attaché, I overheard an Australian (of all people) say: "There's no way I would bring my wife to that mate."

The Times **Marital disharmony** 22 Apr

Sir, Robert Crampton imagines that the score in arguments with his wife of roughly five victories per day for her to one every three years for him is typical of most married couples (Magazine, Beta male, Apr 21). Who knows, either way? However, the score is likely to even out once it is taken into account that, in a marriage, even though you're right you can still be wrong.

DTel **Flannels v Handkerchiefs** 27 Apr

SIR - Whilst serving in the Far East in the days before air conditioning was widespread, it was common to find a pile of laundered coloured flannels in the cloakrooms of officers' messes for use to wipe away perspiration. On hot days, I always have a white one at hand for use instead of a handkerchief to mop my brow.

The Times **A library for worthy women** 28 Apr

Sir, The emotive language of the 50 leading women pleading (letter, 27 Apr) about the decision by London Metropolitan University to "rid itself" of The Women's Library being a "betrayal" - its opening hours being "slashed" to one day a week - is reminiscent of the recent letter which turned out to have been sculpted by a PR company ("Desmond's lottery accuses Camelot of shady tactics", Apr 14).

It transpires that the University's Board of Governors announced last month that they will be seeking a new home, custodian or sponsor of The Women's Library's collections by the end of the year. Only then will the opening hours be reduced from four to one day a week, for a period of three years, before a further review.

Rather than complaining of an "unacceptable threat" to publicly funded research and calling upon the government to intervene, the signatories would seem to be well placed to use their individual and collective imagination and influence to seek out and find potential custodians, or help devise other innovative solutions. Whether or not they look to the Big Society or philanthropy in doing so, they have a big opportunity to demonstrate their worth.

DTel **One code for ministers and one for...** 30 Apr

SIR - Ten years ago I was a member of a project team for a £500m procurement of services for the Ministry of Defence. I was expressly forbidden by junior commercial staff from having lunch in a pub with a former Army colleague who worked for one of the bidders. Being used to the concept of a lawful command, we never did meet, but had we done so, I am now left wondering if I would have committed anything more than a "technical sin"; not least as I was well aware of the code concerning what could not, and so would not, have been discussed ("Pressure growing for Hunt inquiry", April 30).

2012

Daily Telegraph 4 May

Ready for weddings

SIR - C J Wright (Letters, 3 May) asks what relics survive from the days before almost universal casual dress. I have just taken delivery of two new stiff white collars for wear with my morning coats.

The Times **Seeing red** 5 May

Sir, Robert Crampton's omission of redcurrant jelly from his All-Star Cricket Condiment Xl (Beta male, May 5) must surely rank alongside Basil D'Oliveira not being selected for the MCC tour to South Africa in 1968-69 and David Gower for the England tour of India in 1992-93. Outrageous.

The Times 8 May

On the button

Sir, Only a prep school boy dressed by his mother would have the bottom button of a two-button jacket fastened.

THE WIT AND WISDOM OF AN ORDINARY SUBJECT

DTel **Fountain pens on the bench** 8 May

SIR - Tony Matson asks "when did you last see anyone using a fountain pen?" (Letter, May 8). In my case the answer is last month, by a judge on the bench in Reading Crown Court where I was on jury service. The jury was provided with pencils.

DTel **Tesco v Waitrose** 11 May

SIR - With Asda, Sainsbury's, Lidl and Morrisons already there, the people of Malton must have been hoping for a Waitrose.

Sunday Times **Not for the first time** 14 May

Sir, The Ministry of Defence's collective memory is not as good as it should be if it advised the Secretary of State for Defence, Philip Hammond, to say "for the first time in the defence budget we've got a reserve in each year" and "we've also put a sizeable contingency into the equipment plan, which has never been done before" (News, May 13).

Michael Heseltine tried to do just that when he was the Secretary of State for Defence (1983-86), by creating a 10% layer in the ten-year costings of the equipment requirements programme, but it was called a regulator. Inevitably it fell to future savings as the money wasn't committed and, after his departure, it was quietly dropped.

Let's hope that the mechanism will work this time, as even if the defence budget is due to rise above inflation, savings will still be called for when costs rise unaffordably and priorities change.

Col J M C Watson (retd)

Dear Mr Watson,   *29 May*

Thank you for your letter. I had put it aside to publish but there is space for only a fraction of the letters received each week and I'm afraid we were unable to include yours.

Thank you for taking the trouble to write.

Yours sincerely,

Parin Janmohamed
Letters Editor

DTel   **Mils and boom**   19 May

SIR - George Bristow is not entirely correct when he says that all navigation the world over uses a 360-degree compass (Letter, May 19). In the 1950s, NATO countries adopted metric units of measurement for land and general use. Mils (circle/6400) compasses and protractors became standard for land navigation, although degrees remained in use for naval and air purposes, reflecting civil practices.

Private Eye **Pedantry corner –** 22 May
Hunt colours: a guide

There must be dozens of hunts that wear pink coats which Mike Barfield could have used to illustrate his cartoon "Hunt Colours: A Guide" (*Eye 1314)*, but the Berkelely Hunt is not one of them - the Master and hunt servants wear yellow coats.

The Times **Beating the pain** 23 May

Sir, I was beaten in the Fifties and Sixties once each by my father, then my prep school and public school headmasters for what would now indeed be trivial matters (letters, May 22 and 23). Before the last occasion, trials were held in the dormitory using wooden coat hangers against a string vest pulled down under my trousers, which proved most effective the following day.

DTel **Rank awareness** 26 May

SIR - Your obituary of David Metcalfe (May 26) states that "at the end of his three-year commission, he was a second lieutenant", as if he had in some way been promoted during it. An officer is commissioned as a second lieutenant and the next rank up is a lieutenant, which David Metcalfe's particular commission in the Irish Guards would have precluded him from reaching. The rank structure used to be common knowledge, but in spite of the Army currently being in the public eye, it seems to have become too obscure, even for many pub quizzes today.

| *DTel* | **What's in a name** | 28 May |

SIR - I have never been particularly keen on the name Malcolm (Letters, May 28) until I noticed how many managed to get their letters published - sometimes two and occasionally three on one day - and not just in the *Telegraph* newspapers.

| *The Times* | **Perhaps non** | 29 May |

Sir, A ringing suggestion from Mike Morrison (letter, May 28), but where I went to school "Notres" was a possessive adjective or pronoun and not a noun - even in English.

| *The Times* | **Even more collective nouns** | 30 May |

Sir, ...and as a collective noun for a group of ladies such as those used to illustrate "Bishops, women and

THE WIT AND WISDOM OF AN ORDINARY SUBJECT

the Church of England" (letters, May 30), how about a Vision?

DTel   **BBC staff beyond homework**   5 Jun

SIR - I was beginning to think that the BBC 1 commentary on the Diamond Jubilee Concert was going to be even worse than it had been on the Thames pageant (Letters, June 5), when I noticed I was watching the BBC News Channel. Talk of the Duchess of Wessex, the Second Battalion Coldstream Guards and the Queen being our longest reigning monarch, is unlikely to be improved by homework if the BBC engages staff who so obviously don't know what they are talking about in the first place. But as the news channel's output is also heading for foreign audiences, perhaps they think it doesn't really matter.

DTel   **Other countries can and do**   7 Jun

SIR - Let us not get too carried away with the suggestion that "no other country in the world does it better" (Letters, June 7). I have attended parades and events put on by other countries which, in scale and precision, make Trooping the Colour look like turning out the guard. We do not have a monopoly on organisational skills, but what British-based occasions are is unique, enabling us all to feel pride in our nation and for it to stand tall amongst all others.

| *DTel* | **Twinning of towns** | 9 Jun |

SIR - I once stayed at a place called King of Prussia in Pennsylvania. If it is looking for a twin, I can think of nowhere more fitting than Dumfries, home of Queen of the South.

| *Sunday Telegraph* | | 10 Jun |

Second-class specials

SIR - Clifford Webb writes that second-class postage seems not to benefit from commemorative stamps (Letters, June 3).

Had his local village post office opted to sell them, from May 31 he would have found a stamp book that includes two Diamond Jubilee commemoratives with four of the new diamond blue stamps - though admittedly for first-class postage.

Different commemorative designs for second-class postage are produced each Christmas, when they are probably most in demand, but they are valid for use throughout the year.

Sunday Times 10 Jun

Facebook friend

In answer to Elizabeth R Norton's question "Is there, or was there any place in Britain named Barville Park?" (Special edition of May 31, 1953, last week), it is at Armadale, between Edinburgh and Glasgow. In keeping with the times, the details can only be found on Facebook.

DTel **Memoirs are made of this** 13 Jun

SIR - The police is not the first service for its senior ranks to be disgruntled when hearing that such a senior appointment "will not be recruited from its members" (Leading article, June 13).

When Sir Percy Sillitoe went from a distinguished police background to become the Director-General of MI5 in 1946 he was faced with similar opposition, but went on to be the first DG to publish his memoirs, *Cloak without Dagger*, in 1955.

I hope that Tom Winsor is confirmed as the next Chief Inspector of Constabulary and I look forward to reading his memoirs in due course.

| *The Oldie* | **Pedants revolt** | 16 Jun |

Madam, I have just heard Norman Smith, Chief Political Correspondent, say on BBC Television News that the country is "in the middle of a double-dip recession". How on earth does he know that? Unless he knows when it will end, which he won't, he can't possibly know with such certainty when we are in the middle of it.

| *The Times* | **A gem by the beach** | 17 Jun |

Sir, Thanks are due to Alastair Sawday for not listing the Rashleigh Arms, Polkerris, Cornwall - a gem by the beach - as one of "30 great pubs for summer" (Weekend pullout, June 16); though I'd be happy to share this information with readers of the letters pages.

| *DTel* | **Olympic cricketers** | 17 Jun |

SIR - If the opening ceremony of the Olympic Games is to be held under intensive lighting and noise (Letter, June 16), then perhaps the cricketers should be dressed in coloured pyjamas and not whites. And unless they are to be portrayed by people who can actually play the game, then they too would be better represented by models.

THE WIT AND WISDOM OF AN ORDINARY SUBJECT

STel **New second-class stamps** 20 Jun

SIR - How fitting that Clifford Webb asking for more commemorative stamps for second-class postage (Letter, June 3) should have been answered with the issue of one on Tuesday depicting Mr Bumble from Oliver Twist.

DTel **Enoch Powell –** 21 Jun
women are not clubbable

SIR - At his talk to the Joint Service Defence College at Greenwich in 1986 and no doubt elsewhere, Enoch Powell made much of his contention, about membership of the House of Commons, that women were not clubbable. Even though the proportion of women MPs there has more than trebled since then and clubs such as MCC have allowed women to be elected as members, I am left to imagine him arguing eloquently that, even so, they have not become any more clubbable.

DTel **Winning – home or away** 23 Jun

SIR - E L Firth writes that "in 1948 the England football team beat the world champions Italy 0-4 in Turin" (Letter, June 23). But surely England beat Italy 4-0, wherever it was played?

| *Private Eye* | **Pink coats** | 24 Jun |

….Just to put Tony Hastings' pedantry to bed (Eye 1316): hunting coats were made by an 18th century tailor called Mr Pink and not the modern day outfitter (Thomas) Pink's of Jermyn Street; and even if the scarlet coats in the cartoon (Apparently, Eye 1314) had been made by a Pink, Steve Tilley was correct to point out that the Berkeley huntsman's coat should have been yellow (Eye, 1315).

| *The Times* | **Captain's dress sense** | 24 Jun |

Sir, I was saddened to read of Ed Smith's time as captain of Middlesex in his entertaining piece ("Dressed up or down, we are what we wear", Opinion, June 23) on several counts. If ever there were a game where individuality is likely to be beneficial and the captain's leadership is as important off the field of play as on it, then it is cricket.

For the South African coach to have the final say about what the players wore travelling to away matches says something about their relative positions, but for it to be shellsuits and trainers was not just dressing down, but dressing at the bottom. As the coach lasted only half a season, I hope that a return to sartorial self-expression restored some self-respect to them as cricketers and a team.

Sunday Times 24 Jun

(Sports letters)

How wonderful it was to read that the "three Ws" - Sir Frank Worrell, Sir Everton Weekes and Sir Clyde Walcott - have been joined by the Rev Wesley Winfield Hall, the great West Indian fast bowler of the 1950s and 60s, as a knight in the Queen's birthday honours.

DTel **Mistaken date –** 26 Jun
cricket and the weather

SIR - David Sherman may well have been at Lord's for the Saturday of the Test between England and the West Indies in 1976 when it was completely rained off (Letters, June 25), but it was not on June 23 – my wife's birthday – it was June 19. We were married three years later on a Saturday in May, one of the few on which I hadn't played cricket since the age of eight. However, I didn't miss a game, as it rained; though it did brighten up later on.

DTel   **Not all Scots speak**   2 Jul
with a Scottish accent

SIR - A H N Gray's observation that every fifth person he passes in any street in Scotland speaks with an English accent (Letters, July 3) reminds me of Patrick Cargill's character of Dr McTaggart who replied to Tony Hancock in *The Blood Donor* in the Queen's English: "Well, we're not all Rob Roys".

The Times   **Principles and assumptions**   3 Jul

Sir, With due respect to the eleven bishops putting down their pre-Synod marker, "that it is the will of the majority that women should be ordained as bishops" (letter, July 3) is not a principle, but an assumption. A principle would be that the will of the majority be enacted.

The Times   7 Jul

Making cuts work

Sir, It is reassuring to read that the Chief of the General Staff is confident that Army 2020 will be imaginatively configured and properly resourced to meet the future demands of this uncertain world ("The new Army won't be fighting the old wars", Opinion, July 5).

However, similar imagination went into the reconfiguration of our armoured divisions in Germany in 1978, when the brigade level of command was to be dispensed with and two tank regiments and three infantry battalions put under the direct command of each division - exactly what is now proposed, but for armoured brigades. When it was realised that the span of command was too great – in peace and in war - brigade headquarters were reintroduced.

If the span of command was too great for a defensive force already in place, it will surely be too great for an expeditionary one under lower level and less well resourced headquarters. It is widely recognised that the optimum span of command at all levels is three; five was not viable before and it is most unlikely to be in the future.

COL MALCOLM WATSON (RET'D)

DTel	**Lords vote dropped**	10 Jul

SIR - This is democracy in action, in spite of no votes being cast.

DTel	**Top tips for broccoli stalks left in supermarkets**	12 Jul

SIR - Dipping a trimmed broccoli stalk into ink sees it rise up the stalk. If supermarkets were to give the stalks left by customers (Letters, July 12) to their meat suppliers, they could provide an environmentally friendly and sustainable supply of marker pens to use on their animals, though the ink would need to be permanent.

DTel	**Not Sunningdale, but Wentworth**	14 Jul

SIR - The photograph of golf at Sunningdale ("Life in the London fast lane", *Telegraph* magazine, July 14) is in fact of Wentworth - a most unfortunate substitution.

Some years ago, I was being driven though Sunningdale to play at Wentworth by a member there, when he told me that Sunningdale members referred to Wentworth as Egham Municipal.

Enquiring if there was a counter-insult, I was regaled with the tale of a gentleman playing at Sunningdale, who went to see the Secretary in his office and wondered if he might be able to cash a cheque. Asked if he was member and admitting that he was not, the Secretary said: "Well that'll be all right then".

Daily Telegraph   16 Jul

Ban on wedding bands

SIR - I keep in my briefcase an inexpensive wrist watch with two dials (Letters, July 14); the larger one I set for the time here. I use it when making and expecting transatlantic telephone calls, setting the smaller dial to the time zone concerned.

The Times   **HSBC – cheques and balances**   18 Jul

Sir, The BBC's Washington Correspondent, reporting on television about the latest humiliation to hit British banks ("HSBC was used to 'clean drugs money'", report, July 18), said that the US Senate had found that HSBC "had essentially allowed money-laundering to take place, or had not put in enough checks and balances to try and prevent it". Unless I have misunderstood the latter term and misspelt the former, then this is nothing to do with balances and all about checks, which have clearly been inadequate and is another shocking revelation about current banking practices.

Sunday Times **Thumbs-down to thumbs-down** 18 Jul

My youngest daughter laughed out loud when she saw the thumbs-down signs throughout the Olympic Scrapbook (*Sunday Times/The Times* enclosure, July 15). The thumbs-up sign in social media means "like it" and so a thumbs-down sign was more likely to mean "bin it" than "stick it here". Perhaps a picture of a glue stick would have been better.

DTel **Two-way roundabout** 19 Jul

SIR - Traffic goes both ways around the roundabout at the independence monument in Mexico City (Letters, July 19). Motorists have been known to circle several times before being able to achieve their preferred exit.

DTel **Throwing some light on lining curtains** 22 Jul

SIR - Charles Moore suggests, as an example, that lining curtains for the NHS is not one of the services that the state should provide ("Business and government have learnt each other's worst habits", Comment, July 21) and who could possibly disagree? However, no one should imagine that curtains in the public sector – where they exist and however they are procured - will be lined, as they are only there to provide some privacy and not to keep the light out.

DTel/ Sunday Times **Defiant joy is unsporting** 24/25 Jul

SIR - What a contrast between the winning smile of Bradley Wiggins ("The hero who did it without his Dad", Features, July 24) and Daryl Steyn's defiant and unbecoming display of joy at taking 5 wickets (First Investec Test, Sport, July 24) in South Africa's crushing defeat of England. A magnanimous smile would equally have drawn the congratulations of Steyn's team mates in the middle and done much more on television to cement his position as the No 1 bowler in the world in the eyes of cricketers at all levels. Let's hope we see winners smiling with joy during the Olympics.

The Times **Unhealthy associations** 25 Jul

Sir, The pleading signaturies, citing Sachin Tendulkar's tie-up with Coca-Cola, in their case against the successful promotion of unhealthy junk food by well-loved sportsmen and women (letter, July 25), may be able to take heart from his previous role as a Global Ambassador for the Royal Bank of Scotland in their 2008 campaign: "Make it happen".

The Times **The truth that rarely gets heard** 28 Jul

Sir, Elizabeth Oakley states that doctors in their field know that one in 100 people is born with some biological characteristics of both genders (letters, July 28). They also know that the life expectancy within some of the groups she mentions is reduced by their practice of "a variety of sexual behaviour and preferences". The government preaches almost daily that our lives will be shortened by eating too much junk food, drinking more alcohol than is good for us, smoking tobacco and taking drugs. It is time that doctors of medicine entered the debate on gay issues and gay marriage.

The Oldie **To blazes with fashion** 31 Jul

SIR: Properly tailored blazers, of whatever weight of cloth, which "still feature at many blue riband sporting events as a dress code for spectators in the posh seats" (Fashion, Oldie, August 2012), will be double-breasted and certainly not have family, or any other crests on their breast pockets. Instead, the buttons will convey discretely the appropriate association and, in some circles, no doubt reflecting their nautical origins, blazers will still be referred to as boating jackets.

DTel   **Devoted royal couple**   1 Aug

SIR - In the BBC *News at Ten* item about the silver medal winning performance by Great Britain's three-day event team, Huw Edwards read that "amongst those watching were Prince William and (pause) the Duchess of Cambridge". In case the BBC have forgotten, they broadcast their marriage to the world last year. To the rest of us, the Duke and Duchess of Cambridge still appear to be a devoted couple.

DTel   **School sandwiches**   2 Aug

SIR - Bacon sandwiches at prep school (Letter, August 2) - what luxury! We had dripping at mine.

DTel   **By-elections gains were**   4 Aug
                 important political contests

SIR - Whilst Charles Moore may consider that Boris Johnson is the only Tory since 1992 to have won any important political contest ("Is Boris serious? When it comes to No 10, the answer is deadly so", Opinion,

August 4), MPs Edward Timpson and Chloe Smith – now Economic Secretary to the Treasury - may not agree with him.

They made the only two by-election gains for the Conservatives during the period, overturning 7000 and 5500 majorities in 2008 and 2009 respectively. At the time, the results were variously described as phenomenal, remarkable, convincing, significant and historic.

The winners will understandably remember these by-elections as important political contests as well.

The Times **A different test for G4S** 7 Aug

Sir, I was very sorry to read of Mike Thomas's intimidating experience during the first South Africa Test at the Oval with his wife and son (letter, August 7), which was quite different from the enjoyable time I spent at the second Test at Headingley on Sunday with two daughters, in spite of a day's play cut short by rain.

What was curious, though not intimidating, was the large number of G4S security personnel deployed for a half-filled stadium, who might just have been employed more appropriately at sell-out Olympics venues, allowing some of the servicemen and women who had to replace them to have a day off duty.

THE WIT AND WISDOM OF AN ORDINARY SUBJECT

The Times **Doubly wrong** 11 Aug

Sir, Your chief football correspondent, Oliver Kay, born 15 years after England won the World Cup in 1966, is mistaken if he thinks that "football cannot unite the country like the Olympics can" ("Football has taken a kicking, and it's not fair play", Thunderer, Aug 11).

Like millions of others, I watched the final live on BBC television and in black and white - in my case after a cricket match had been abandoned for rain - and I can assure him that it did. And if Wayne Rooney, as a victorious Olympic boxer swore down the camera, I would not laugh - certainly double standards, but different ones either side of the lens.

DTel **Not old enough** 14 Aug

SIR - I enjoy reading James Hughes-Onslow's column on memorial services in *The Oldie* magazine, but it sometimes appears that he is not old enough to understand what he thinks he hears at them (Letters, August 14). His latest reports that Earl Kitchener of Khartoum, 1919-2011, "applied for National Service during the war".

2012

| *Sunday Times* | **Foregoing extras** | 15 Aug |
| (In gear) | **is nothing new** | |

Sir, I was interested to read that drivers are turning their backs on luxury extras to see what is foregone in trading down from a £24,075 to a £7,195 car (Driving, August 11). I did this some years ago when I discovered "The Garage Your Friends Recommend".

My most recent purchases from them have been a 2001 Renault Espace, with remote central locking, air-conditioning and CD radio (four speakers), for £1000 a year ago; and my 1995 four-door Ford Fiesta LX, with none of the above, for £500 five years ago.

I expect them each to meet my over 12,000 miles a year requirements and those of the Ministry of Transport for the foreseeable future, after which l shall trade them in.

| *DTel* | **Kingdom to come** | 17 Aug |

SIR - If Scotland leaves the UK, I suggest that GBR then competes in future Olympics as YAR - Yorkshire and The Rest.

| *DTel* | **Ladies of the house** | 18 Aug |

SIR - My brother, a chartered accountant, refers to his three daughters as "Numbers 1, 2 and 3 cost-centres".
Jane Watson

Evening Standard 19 Aug

A-levels results aren't the full story

How can it be front page news that there has been a drop in the number taking modern languages at A-level - dramatically so in German and French? Surely the data should have been compiled and made available for analysis and any action necessary last year, following entries to the subjects concerned.
J M C Watson, Berkshire

DTel/Guardian   **A new verb for 2012**   21/30 Aug

SIR - I should like to propose a new verb following the success of the London Olympics 2012 and the revival of "to medal" and "to podium" from the Sydney Olympics (Letters, 19 and 21 September 2000). It is "to clegg". Whilst the noun is the name of a slow, quiet-flying and stealthy bug with a painful bite, the verb means to apply the kiss of Death - as in promoting a supposed benefit in the name of democracy, which will fail through lack of support from those who have a vote on it.

2012

| *The Times* | **Not for stacking** | 22 Aug |

Sir, The dimpled variety with handles could also be class glasses (letters, Aug 22) as they don't stack.

| *The Times* | **What's in a name 2** | 23 Aug |

Sir, I have never been particularly keen on the name Malcolm until I noticed how many managed to get their letters published. The Julians now seem to be in the ascendency (letters, 21, 22, 23 Aug).

| *DTel* | **Choices, choices** | 24 Aug |

SIR - Dr Helena Brown asks what A-levels she should advise her students to take in order to be accepted to read "tableware design", "windsurfing science" and "adventure science" (Letters, August 23). As they are all what could be described as Mickey Mouse subjects, Film Studies would provide a good grounding for all three. The windsurfing and adventure sciences should consider any two from Astronomy, Geography, Spanish and Fashion Design, whilst those going for the tableware option might like to augment Design & Technology with Psychology.

THE WIT AND WISDOM OF AN ORDINARY SUBJECT

The Times   **Failure of the**   1 Sep
Church of England

Sir, What is additionally shocking about the "appalling history" uncovered in the Chichester diocese during the archiepiscopal visitation ordered by the Archbishop of Canterbury, is that it is the first such visit for more than 100 years ("Don't see children without chaperone, clergy told", Aug 31).

In offering his apologies to the victims, Dr Williams says that they were "let down by those they ought to have been able to trust". His lasting legacy to the Church of England should now be to enshrine in its workings a culture of regular episcopal visits at appropriate levels.

In the words of President Ronald Regan, in another context: "Trust but verify".

DTel   **Oh my God**   4 Sep

SIR - Only one of the eight young contestants from Oxford and Cambridge colleges on Monday night's University Challenge was able to identify correctly the opening words of any of four well-known hymns from the music clues - and he wasn't sure of that either. If their generation can't recognise *Guide Me O Thou Great Redeemer, Abide with Me, Dear Lord and Father of Mankind* and *The Lord's My Shepherd*, then what does that tell us about their lives so far and what might uplift them in the future?

2012

The Times	**No fake poodle**	6 Sep

Sir, It was indeed rude for the MP, Brian Binley, to call the Prime Minister Nick Clegg's chambermaid ("Obstacles removed. Now get on and govern", Opinion, Sept 5). However, following Mr Clegg's proposals for the House of Lords, it was the Prime Minister that acted as the watchdog of the constitution.

Private Eye	**Commentatorballs**	6 Sep

"The car itself also had many gunshot wounds."
IMOGEN FOULKES, BBC 1 News,

The Times	**Name of the game**	8 Sep

Sir, What with Swanny, Belly, Trotty, Broady – though not Priory – Straussy and Cooky ("James Anderson is ready to take on increased responsibility under Cook", Cricket, Sept 7), it looks like a name change may be the best way for Kevin Pietersen to get back into the England cricket team.

DTel	**Reduced to this**	8 Sep

SIR - For inadvertent rhymesters, it has to be: "He's a poet / And doesn't know it".

The Times **Sealing the changes** 12 Sep

Sir, In advance of the latest series of learned comments about the office of Lord Chancellor (letters, Sept 12), it was notified in the Court Circular (Register, Sept 11) that "The Rt Hon Christopher Grayling MP took the Oath of Office as Lord Chancellor and Secretary of State for Justice, kissed hands on his appointment and received the Great Seal and the Seal of Office". This would seem to put an end to whether the office of Lord Chancellor might be vacant.

In respect of the contention of Francis Bennion QC that, if it were relevant in a case before it, a higher court would hold that Mr Cameron's recommendation of Mr Grayling was in breach of statute and therefore void, section 2 of the Constitutional Reform Act 2005 – to reinforce the point made by Professor Zellick QC (letter, Sept 6) – makes it clear that the Prime Minister in assessing qualification by experience may take into account *any* of these: experience as a minister, a Member of Parliament, a practising lawyer, an academic lawyer, or other experience that Prime Minister considers relevant. It is difficult therefore to imagine a court agreeing that the recommendation was invalid and contravened the rule of law.

And if, as Michael Beloff QC suggests, the title of Lord Chancellor is to be abolished, what will become of the Great Seal for which he is also the Lord Keeper? The demise of one Great Office of State should not preclude the emergence of another. To the suggestions that some of the duties of the Lord Chancellor could pass to the President of the Supreme Court should be added those that go with the custody and administration of the Great Seal of the Realm, which signifies authorisation of the monarch to implement the advice of the government.

The creation of a new great office with a suitable title in the reign of this monarch would be a worthy legacy of her Diamond Jubilee year.

Evening Standard **Unfortunate editing** 12 Sep

It was unfortunate editing to have Prince William purporting to say "I'd like to have two children with Kate" (News, Sept 12) as if he was expecting to have other children with someone else.
J M C Watson

DTel **Soaps in short cuts** 13 Sep

SIR - Another feature of soap operas (Letters, September 10, 11, 12) is that the scenes are invariably of the same unchallenging length. The same applies to Downton Abbey. Try timing them.

The Times   **Shock research finding**   14 Sep

Sir, So researchers at Groningen University in the Netherlands believe that their study shows that sexual arousal in men "will act to facilitate engagement in pleasurable sex" ("How sexual arousal helps avoid the 'yuk' factor, Science News, Sept 14). Well there's an earth-moving discovery for mankind then.

Daily Telegraph   18 Sep

Milk and lobsters

SIR - I visited Cuba in the Nineties, when fresh milk was not available, but lobster was plentiful.

As the accredited defence attaché visiting from Mexico City, I used to take in my baggage nine waxed cartons of milk for the freezer in the ambassador's residence in Havana. The space was filled on the return flight with lobsters packed in polystyrene.

2012

DTel **Not so, Your Grice** 19 Sep

SIR - Had Elizabeth Grice not slipped up in reporting that the Duchess of Rutland's husband became the 11th Duke and not Earl in 1999 ("One wing for you, one wing for me", September 18), she might have been minded to refer to the bedrooms at fictional Downton Abbey as Belvoiresque rather than the other way round.

The Times **Guardian readers?** 23 Sep

Sir, Matthew Parris asks (Opinion, Sept 22) how many readers must have frowned at the Guardian report "Tory Treasurer wants UK to become more like a tax haven". Not very many, I would suggest, myself included, until I read Nicky Samengo-Turner's letter (Sept 22) and then found the article online. But frown, no – smile, yes.

Daily Telegraph **Sensitivity in uniform** 25 Sep

SIR - And the plural of "pleb" is "plebes" (Letters, September 25), which is what first-year cadets are called at the US military academy West Point, where taking offence is unlikely to see progression to second-year "yuks".

THE WIT AND WISDOM OF AN ORDINARY SUBJECT

STel   **1944 Education Act and 11-plus**   25 Sep

SIR - Lynn Harrison makes a valid point about the 11-plus exam system (Letters, September 23) which, if true, indicates unfairness to girls who were denied a place at grammar schools in place of boys who achieved lower marks. However, this was a meritocratic dilemma for the government of the day and Dr Bruce Denness was not wrong in saying (Letters, September 16) that the system was "totally democratic", as RA Butler's bill had to pass through the elected House of Commons before becoming the 1944 Education Act.

The Times   **Show us your prices**   29 Sep

Sir, The Cask Report on real ale shows some encouraging rising percentages for the brewing industry ahead of Cask Ale Week (Dashboard, Business, Sept 28). It would be a welcome by-product if those pubs taking part in the week were to lead by example and increase the low percentage of premises currently meeting their obligations to display prominently sufficient information about their prices. Less stringent than the legal requirements before 2008, too many landlords are tardy in complying.

The Times 29 Sep

Out of position

Sir, I gave up any pretence at following football when the names of players' positions on the pitch and the shirt numbers associated with them no longer bore any resemblance to what I expected the players to do.

I think I know who would win between today's Premier League teams and their First Division predecessors (letter, Sept 26), but I expect they would be high-scoring matches as neither side's players would know who they were supposed to be marking.

The Cricketer Oct issue

The Snake Games

Policing the snakes of plastic beer glasses during Test matches can be done by embracing an inter-venue competition, heats being sponsored by local brewery partners. The action takes place after play and practising would not be permitted so that few risk ejection for a chance of glory later. A decider is held at Lord's during the Village Cup Final in September. As such, it would be a rival to the County Mascots Race on T20 Finals Day as something to look forward to in the cricket calendar. Step forward a national brewery with some rules and a trophy.

DTel **Identity in France** 1 Oct

SIR - When I give my surname in France the reaction is invariably: "Ah! Sherlock 'olmes."

The Times 6 Oct

Tales of Pudsey

Sir, Annette Anderson from Monaco has no doubt that there are some "over-the-top" people in Pudsey (letter, Oct 5); I suspect the opposite may be true. Why else would

Michael Palin have made frequent references to Pudsey in *Ripping Yarns,* his satirised over-the-top *Boys' Own* adventures, if the people from there were not so understated?

| *The Times* | **Military losses** | 8 Oct |

Sir, The potential loss to the British military of a BAE merger (Leading article, Oct 8) is nothing compared to the actual loss to BAE of the British military, even when the contracts are mutually beneficial (letter, Oct 6).

| *DTel* | **Work suitable for prisons** | 11 Oct |

SIR - Not enough of our prison population being in work begs the question about what work might be suitable (Letters, October 11). Manufacturing hand-held power tools may not be conducive to reducing reoffending rates, but operating call-centres would seem to offer opportunities for education as well as employment, whilst helping the Government bring outsourced operations of business back to Britain. There must be other suggestions worth considering.

THE WIT AND WISDOM OF AN ORDINARY SUBJECT

DTel **Peeling skills are for watching** 16 Oct

SIR - Peeling a mango efficiently (Letters, October 16) is best demonstrated, not described in writing. Searching for "how to cut a mango" on the internet reveals a number of video clips showing clear easy-to-follow techniques.

DTel **Women-only clubs** 17 Oct

SIR - N T P Murphy wonders why women-only clubs have not lasted as long as their male equivalents (Letters, October 17). The late Enoch Powell used to tell his lecture audiences that women were not clubbable. Also, having obtained prized voting rights with membership, they presumably voted to close them if they didn't attract enough members to be viable.

The Times **Day/night darts** 19 Oct

Sir, Alastair Cook's England side should have plenty of time to play darts by day as well as in the evenings on their forthcoming "long" tour to India (Cricket, October 19) as they are playing cricket on only 40 days of their 95-day tour, which includes 10 days back at home.

DTel   **Umpired out**   21 Oct

SIR - I do hope that Janet Armstrong had a second malt loaf to put in her fridge to provide 13 slices for the opposition team and the umpires, as important for a cricket match as a good tea (Letters, October 20).

The Times   **Lives remembered**   23 Oct

Tony Pawson

Malcolm Watson writes: Your obituary of Tony Pawson (October 19) reminded me of a report he filed in the 1970s about a Cambridge University match in which an opening batsman, hoping to get a Blue, had dropped three catches in one innings. He recalled advice he had heard in his playing days and which I have never forgotten: "If you drop a catch, don't worry about it; concentrate on catching the next one. If you drop a second catch, don't worry about it; concentrate on catching the next one. If you drop a third catch, don't worry about it, because you won't be asked to play again."

The opener wasn't picked again, but he did get a Blue for golf.

The Times **Real men own bakeries** 22 Oct

Sir, In the comfortable and leafy North Ferriby of my childhood in the Fifties, where the sweetshop near my grandparents' home was called Rumbelow's (letter, Oct 22), cooks baked and men ran the local East Riding family bakery business Wm Jackson & Son, still baking to perfection and saving the fifth generation's wives the trouble.

The Times **Recipes for disaster** 23 Oct

Sir, Richard Stevenson is right about "ten easy fish recipes" from J Sheekey being far from easy to make (letter, October 16). This Saturday, *The Times* Magazine gave the recipes for four fish dishes made simple in its series titled "The Only Four Recipes You'll Ever Need". I look forward to the series appearing in "The Only Recipe Book You'll Ever Need".

DTel, **Greatest must be unbeaten** 24 Oct

SIR - Brigadier Gerard was undoubtedly a great horse (Letters, October 24), but John Brigham omitted to mention that it was once beaten during its 18 race career, not something on the record of what most people would expect of a horse held to be the greatest, whatever the other criteria.

Back in 1913, the Irish thoroughbred The Tetrarch won all 7 of its starts as a 2-year-old (2yo), but did not race again due to injury. Described by the National Racehorse Museum as a "phenomenon" and voted 2yo of the 20th Century, the United States National Sporting Library goes even further, describing The Tetrarch as "probably the greatest 2yo of all time" and "possibly the greatest runner ever".

However, he was not the greatest looking horse, being gangly and having a grey coat sprinkled with white blotches and lime green spots, hence known as "the Spotted Wonder".

The Times   **Probably not**   25 Oct

Sir, If ever there were a need for an understanding and application of probability theory, it is in "the maintenance of a state of readiness during every hour of the day and night to deal with anything and everything, even to the extent that this may restrict the scope for preventive policing" as a valid priority (letters, Oct 25).

DTel　　　　　　**Fowl for Christmas**　　　26 Oct

SIR - John Parker has a point (Letters, October 26); but is it ever proper to use proper nouns as verbs, or can we really be minded to say here that Christmas has been Fowlered?

The Guardian　　　**Enlightening**　　　27 Oct
　　　　　　　　building regulation

Thirty years ago I was responsible for identifying and promoting realistic, but low-cost, solutions to alterations in requirements for soldiers' living accommodation in Germany; we were frequently thwarted by different interpretations of fire regulations at various levels of authority ("Government orders building standards review", News, October 26).

The general responsible for Army Quartering (as it was then called) suggested, to no avail, that trained soldiers should be able to escape from the first floor of buildings, without the need for expensive fire escapes. Now that soldiers currently stationed there are to be brought back to UK, adoption of such a suggestion for purpose-built accommodation could help MoD make best use of its budget and at the same time lead the way in stimulating activity in the economy and drive job creation in the construction industry.

Suitably positioned ropes and poles should be quite adequate for the purpose.

Private Eye **Savile inquiry** 27 Oct

Surely it must have been in the BBC's interests to have appointed Lord Saville to look into its present difficulties.

Evening Standard **Joining up the circle** 27 Oct

I went to London on Saturday to attend a wine fair in Westminster. To get there from Paddington by tube took twice as long as it should have done as the Circle line was not operating; though there were too few indications that this was the case. Trains on the District line still carried visible and audio messages for changes onto the Circle line to be made at intermediate stations. In this age of programmed electronic communications, such a lack of joined-up operating capability was irritating at best for out-of-town visitors, but must have been quite bewildering for the many patient foreigners using the overcrowded alternative routes. We both deserved better.
J M C Watson

DTel **Dying unnaturally** 29 Oct

SIR - I was surprised to read that Mr Howells, 48, had died of natural causes due to alcohol poisoning ("Pub landlord's dilemma over body in the gents", News, October 29). Surely this was as unnatural a death by misadventure (accident following a wilful and dangerous risk) as can be imagined in any rational understanding of drinking to excess, never mind the circumstances, if not by the coroner.

DTel **Unpublished shades** 30 Oct

SIR - Ian Hollingshead is unlikely to be short of suggestions for titles for future compilations of unpublished *Telegraph* readers' letters (Features, October 31); for me the colour of the dust jacket is also eagerly awaited. After pale shades of blue, yellow and green, I had expected salmon pink for *Imagine My Surprise...*, but mauve it is. Perhaps next year - though, please, not a shade of grey.

The Times 30 Oct

War games

Sir, Allan Mallinson ("The vision for the new Territorials must be radical", Register,

Oct 27) repeats the words of Philip Hammond, the Defence Secretary: "We're not interested in reservists who want to play at being a soldier. It will be a serious commitment", without addressing the issue of whether 30,000 part-time soldiers will be serving in 2020.

It is quite possible to be a serious soldier and enjoy *most of** what that entails. If the commitment is not enjoyable, there will not be enough reservists to play with, now or in 2020.

COL MALCOLM WATSON (RET'D)

*Edited later for the record by The Times. See next letters.

The Times   **A cut too far**   2 Nov

Sir, Allan Mallinson explains (letter, Nov 1) that a sentence was cut from his article ("The vision for the new Territorials must be radical", Register, Oct 27) due to pressure on space and the sentence was then included as part of his letter. In my letter of Oct 30, which he agreed with, one sentence should have read: "It is quite possible to be a serious soldier and enjoy *most of* what that entails". As a result of this omission, a flippant insult to all soldiers was posted

in *The Times* online. I hope that space might now be available to publish this sentence in full.
COL MALCOLM WATSON (RET'D)

Dear Colonel Watson,   *2 Nov*

Please accept my sincere apology for the way in which your letter was edited for publication. Clearly the words "most of" should not have been removed from that sentence during the editing process.

We have now corrected the sentence in the online record of the Letters pages:

http://www.thetimes.co.uk/tto/opinion/letters/article3583397.ece

Yours sincerely,

Jeremy Vine
Assistant Editor, The Register
The Times
3 Thomas More Square
London E98 1TT

What's Brewing   Nov issue

Keg buster retire?

I was disappointed to read another letter implying that Keg Buster should move on (Game for a laugh, *WB Oct*). Since joining CAMRA in 1976, I have always turned to Bill Tidy's cartoon strip first. It would be a tragedy if it were jettisoned before the artist himself decides to call it a day.

However, as you report that cask ale now outsells keg, perhaps KB's work has finally paid off and has earned him a comfortable retirement. If that happened to occur next year, 2013 would also be a suitable year to publish a third volume of Keg Buster cartoons (following those published in 1981 and 1997). It could even be a bumper volume, suitably supported by CAMRA.

The Cricketer **Star letter** Nov issue

No spleen to vent

Your subtitle to the Letters pages is "Spleens, vented" yet I don't have one. As a matter of fact, nor does Geoffrey Boycott. In 1973 Geoffrey and I put on 150 (99 and 44 not out) for the first wicket in a match at Pateley Bridge during the Nidderdale Show, the annual Yorkshire dales agricultural event. I wonder if there is a spleenless partnership that exceeds our own.

Daily Telegraph 3 Nov

We've got it taped

SIR - I still have cassette tapes in my K-registered car (Letters, November 2), but have been unable to find anyone to repair a favourite one. Luckily, I recently found a CD of it, and have transferred it to tape for my continued enjoyment.

The Times 5 Nov

Countdown begins on extra airport capacity

Sir, I cannot agree with your leading article that the decision to be taken on extra airport capacity is at least as important as the bold one taken on the Olympics. It is far more important, but needs to be equally bold.

DTel **My Phuey!** 7 Nov

SIR - My father, aged 92, and step-mother, 86, have a number of mobile phones which they do not use, some still in their packaging; they have a push-button device using the landline for emergencies. The credit-card sized My Phone ("Phone to cut confusion for the elderly", November 7) looks easy to use, but still has to be found, charged and calls paid for, things which have eluded them so far. A more reliable way for people to "contact nearest and dearest" might be for the small number of personal contacts to call potential My Phone owners on their landlines periodically, at little or no cost to themselves.

DTel   **Tube fares**   9 Nov

SIR - Readers might be interested to know that whilst an Off-Peak Travelcard for unlimited tube and bus journeys in Zones 1-2 now costs £7, the same for Zones 1-6 with a railcard discount costs only £5.60, making my five journeys on Thursday a bargain (Letters, November 8 and 9).

Sunday Telegraph   11 Nov

'Skyfall' stretches credulity with its unfeasible train-top tussle (P)

SIR - I saw in the credits after *Skyfall* that there were two male draughtspersons and one male drapesmaster. Wonderful.

The Times   **Unforced error**   15 Nov

Sir, Your leading article ("Forces for Change", Nov 15) confuses the term "senior level" (inspector), which the Commissioner of the Metropolitan Police, Mr Hogan-Howe, wishes more people to enter the police service at, rather than working their way up the ranks, with the term "senior officers" (captain RN, colonel, group captain and above), whose quality in the Armed Forces it claims has been raised by such an approach. Suitably qualified people can become officers in the Armed Forces without having to serve in the ranks, but those going on to become senior officers will have done so by virtue of their training, ability and experience, which correlate directly with their quality, not this method of entry.

DTel **Executive reminders** 16 Nov

SIR - Signs such as "Putting Patients First" and "Serving the Community" are extracts from organisations' vision and mission statements. They need to be displayed (Letters, November 15) lest highly paid executives forget what was agreed at costly away-days organised to devise them.

The Times **Better seen than unread** 17 Nov

Sir, May I dare to add those Biblical epics to last Saturday's list of films that are better than the book ("25 films that are better than the book", Review, Nov 17): *The Robe, Samson and Delilah, The Ten Commandments* and *Ben-Hur* to name a few. After all, they are likely to be the nearest all but the most devout of future generations will get to any part of the *Bible's* text and can at least bring to life a famous book unread.

DTel   **Newsnight refocused**   20 Nov

SIR - A redeeming feature of last week's output on *Newsnight* was the rolling report on the territorial dispute between China and Japan. In April 1970, I was a young army officer stationed in Hong Kong en route to Japan - for *Expo' 70* - on *HMS Bulwark*. A book doing the rounds on board was *And to My Nephew Albert I Leave the Island What I Won Off Fatty Hagan in a Poker Game*, a most amusing novel set on a tiny island off the coast of Britain, which becomes the focus of the superpowers' armed forces. I do hope that it has been translated and is being read by the oriental navies, giving some perspective to the similar scenario they are acting out in the East China Sea before it becomes a reality.

DTel   **Seeing is healing**   21 Nov

SIR - Tim Stafford Thornton must try to ensure that he gets someone to see him in motion who knows what they are looking at (Letters, November 21). Twenty-five years ago in the USA, I suffered from a bad back for three months, when I was eventually referred to a neurosurgeon. He came out of his office to greet his waiting patients and only had to see me walk towards him to know that I had ruptured a disc and at what level, a diagnosis which led to a successful, though belated, operation and no further trouble.

| *The Times* | **Laity** | 22 Nov |

Sir, To a layman like me, a draft Women Bishops Measure indicates that there could be changes before a final one is agreed. If not, then why was the measure voted on not a final one? And if it was a draft, won't the final measure require another vote? Mediation would seem to provide the opportunity to move from a draft to a final measure that will achieve the two-thirds majority necessary throughout the General Synod in a vote which will then be required ("Anglicans to seek help from mediators", report, Nov 22).

| *Country Life* | **A history lesson not forgotten** | 23 Nov |

Your Town & Country column ("The making of Winston Churchill", November 21) suggests that Blenheim Place was built by John, 1st Duke of Marlborough. When history of the period was still taught at school, I learnt that Blenheim Palace was a gift from Queen Anne and a grateful nation following his famous victory at the Battle of Blenheim in 1704. The reality was more complicated and could warrant an article on its own. However, the clear intention at the time from the inscription on the plaque on the East Gate, which confirms the gift, was that "this house was built for John Duke of Marlborough" and not by him.

THE WIT AND WISDOM OF AN ORDINARY SUBJECT

DTel   **A different type of Bond girl**   25 Nov

SIR - It is a mistake in itself to suppose that those who spot mistakes in films and television series are always looking for them (Leading article, November). It's just that they know about what they are looking at, or hearing, and they point out what is wrong, which advisers on set either don't seem to or are overruled, if they are employed at all.

Mistakes between scenes and takes are a matter of continuity, which used to be handled by "continuity girls", as they were thought to be better than men at preventing these errors. I could not find any form of continuity person listed in the credits after *Skyfall*, and if such mistakes are to be eliminated in future, priority should be given to the search for a competent continuity girl over the next Bond girl.

The Times   **Young drivers in older cars**   25 Nov

Sir, I do hope that the programmable car key that can limit a driver's speed developed by Ford for the Fiesta ("Car key limits younger drivers' speed", News, Nov 24) can be retrofitted to my K-registered model when it becomes the third of my daughters' starter cars. It should also enable insurance companies to restrict any rise in premiums for young drivers driving older cars.

	2012	
The Times	**All in a name**	26 Nov

Sir, Mrs Atkins is mistaken (letter, Nov 27). She can happily remain Mrs Dennis Atkins as a widow and would use her own Christian name if she were a divorcée.

The use of "Mrs Paul Cornish MB BChir 1984 (Cantab) DRCOG DCH MRCGP DFFP" would seem to provide the information she seeks to convey in a formal context; and "Hello, I'm Fiona Cornish" in an informal one (letters, Nov 26, 27).

The Times	**A period of silence in this world and the next**	29 Nov

Sir, The letter (Nov 16) from Prebendary Thomas, Canon Killwick and many others emphasised six times the "draft" nature of the Women Bishops Measure that went before the General Synod, a point noticeably ignored by the Rural Dean of Ipswich in his response (letter, Nov 20), but clearly integral when referred to again by correspondents following the vote against it (letters, Nov 22).

Now, eight who voted against the Measure (letter, Nov 29), far from shedding some light on the matter, write wishing to introduce a "new briefer Measure", which twelve who voted against would then be prepared to vote for.

All this, whilst a friend, local church warden and *Times* reader is dying; I am glad he can't read it. He is not the only one who deserves a period of silence on this matter.

The Times 1 Dec

Rush to judgement

Sir, Professor Stevenson's letter (Nov 30) still begs the question: What is a Canadian? According to a comedian at the Calgary Stampede in 1978, a Canadian is an immigrant with seniority, which received a roar of approval from the audience.

Sunday Telegraph 2 Dec

Sgt Nightingale's case should never have been sent to court (P)

SIR - Jim Cartwright is correct (Letters, November 25) that it is difficult to imagine, in earlier days, that Sgt Nightingale, the SAS sniper recently released after the Court of Appeal reduced his sentence, would ever have been charged with holding a firearm illegally.

If he had been, it would have been within the authority of his commanding officer (CO) to dismiss the charge. That the CO could not do so is the result of over-reaction to some well-publicised cases which led to the withdrawal of this discretion from military justice.

Col Malcolm Watson (retd)

The Times   6 Dec

If you want compassionate nursing, turn the clock back

Sir, Your leading article (Dec 4) says that the report, *Compassion in Practice*, written by Jane Cummings, the Chief Nursing Officer for England, describes exactly what nursing today needs to become. Ms Cummings's six areas for defining good nursing are: care, compassion, competence, communication, courage and commitment. That we have got to a state where such

empirical core values have to form a vision which needs to be launched indicates a profession that has lost contact with its body of knowledge and code of ethics which once defined it. This report has not defined what good nursing must become, it describes what it once was and should always have been.

Ms Cummings's lasting legacy must be that such a decline cannot happen again.

The Times **Lives remembered** 6 Dec

Han Suyin

Malcolm Watson writes: Your obituary of Han Suyin (November 9), which noted the colossal success of the film's title song *Love is a Many Splendoured Thing*, reminded me of an interview I heard the late Jean Metcalfe give on the radio. During her time hosting *Two-Way Family Favourites* she was asked on one occasion to play: "Love is a Very Splendid Thing". She was happy to agree that it certainly was, and then went on to play a version of the actual theme song, which she said was one of the most requested in the life of the programme.

STel	**Dundas Arms**	6 Dec
(Discovery)		

SIR - Fiona Duncan ignores the fact that radio reception for a wide variety of stations was available through the digital television provided at The Dundas Arms, as it will be now at most of "the best places to stay in UK". Her dislike of brown bedroom furniture is clear, but is mistakenly targeted in this case. Brown is matter of taste and is in keeping with the ambience of the place, but horrid it is not and it helps make this place a gem.

Dear Mr Watson,

Thank you for writing. I am sure you will agree that independent critics are entitled to their views about hotel bedrooms, as you are to yours.

With best wishes

Fiona

DTel   **Dave Brubeck**   7 Dec
                       and Mark Twain

SIR - With the publication of the birthday of Dave Brubeck, the jazz musician and composer, opposite his obituary (December 6), it appears that his age of 92 was slightly exaggerated.

The Times   **Ghana's independence**   12 Dec

Sir, It is misleading to say that Ghana declared independence in 1957 ("Democracy in Africa", leading article, Dec 11), which implies there was no consent from the parent state. It was gained as a self-governing realm of the Commonwealth after the Gold Coast had been granted independence by the government of the United Kingdom. The new West African state also incorporated Ashanti, the Northern Territories and Togoland and as such was the first sub-Saharan African nation to achieve independence and celebrate it.

DTel   **Entertaining etiquette**   14 Dec

SIR - What a pleasant change to read something complimentary about Pippa Middleton's book, *Celebrate* (Comment, Notebook, December 14), which has now been remaindered. If, as Mary Kenny says, it is "probably extremely helpful to people who seek to be informed about basic aspects of entertaining" then it would seem to offer good value for money and potential as a text book for etiquette courses such as the one being run at Fowey Community Centre (Comment, "Good manners are oil to our social wheels", December 14).

Sunday Times 16 Dec

(Sports letters)

In Alastair Cook we are surely seeing the next of England's cricketing knights. This wonderful player and role model should in time be honoured like recent Olympians.

DTel **Abuse of animal funds** 18 Dec

SIR - The BBC 1 News item on Monday night linking the Heythrop Hunt (pronounced *Heathrup*, not the BBC's *Haythrop*), the first to be fined for hunting with dogs, with the "so called Chipping Norton set" and the Prime Minister, was as disproportionate as the £327,000 spent by the RSPCA against the £19,000 penalty it secured ("Judge 'staggered' by £330,000 RSPCA case", Report, December 18).

If it was in the public interest for the RSPCA to bring a private prosecution, then it must now be in the public interest for the RSPCA to be held to account for the possible abuse of funds privately donated and deliberately diverted from the costs of the charity's stated principal task "to rescue, rehabilitate and rehome hundreds of thousands of animals each year in England and Wales", the reason why most people donate.

The Times **Chanel for men** 18 Dec

Sir, Has the regular appearance of advertisements in your pages for Chanel No 5 Parfum with a male model and the word INEVITABLE any connection with the current promotion of gay marriage?

DTel **Hunting down the Heythrop** 19 Dec

SIR - William Shawcross, chairman of the Charity Commission, signalled that he would curb the RSPCA's campaigning if it "overstepped the mark" (News report, December 18). Spending £327,000 to secure a £19,000 penalty on the Heythrop Hunt, albeit the first of its kind, would seem to indicate not just over-stepping the mark, but a no-ball of match-fixing proportions.

| *The Times* | **Familiarity does not breed contentment** | 19 Dec |

Sir, I can assure Charlotte Manton (letter, Dec 20) that my sister was very familiar with my Meccano and train sets, and my brother and I with her dolls and toy high-heeled shoes for dressing up; but funnily enough we really liked and preferred playing with the toys we were given. Had we received each others', I expect we would predictably have swopped them for the same reasons - sooner rather than later - and that most children would do the same today.

| *DTel/STel* | **Chichester, the one and only** | 22/26 Dec |

SIR, A question on Mastermind on Friday night began "For which Sussex cathedral.....?". In the history of the programme, is this the smallest number of words needed to provide the answer?

| *The Times* | **Nonsensical to many** | 26 Dec |

Sir, If, as your leading article says ("Ever Closer Union", Dec 26), it is a non sequitur to define marriage as "the love of husband and wife, which is creative of new human life", which itself cannot be part of what constitutes the purpose of marriage, then why does the established marriage ceremony say that it is ordained first for the procreation of children, or similar words?

If ever there were a non sequitur to the arguably unacknowledged majority, it is surely that "The argument that marriage is in crisis and needs support is unexceptionable" is not followed by your suggestion that "One way of supporting it is to enhance its legitimacy by extending it to same-sex couples."

DTel　　　　　　**Downton observer**　　　　　28 Dec

SIR - As the German psychologist, Hermann Ebbinghaus, lived until 1909, it is possible that his findings about a "learning curve" could have been reported in the *Yorkshire Observer* (Letters, December 28). However, the copy being read in the Christmas episode of *Downton Abbey* would have to have survived since before 1904, when the weekly newspaper's name became the *Yorkshire News*.

The Times　　　　　**Ironic water**　　　　　28 Dec

Sir, Neither my edition of *The Oxford Dictionary of Quotations* nor any of the sources I have consulted on line seem to support G. Bernard Shaw and Stephen Gibbs-Sier (letters. Dec 24 and Dec 28); though on the internet their preferred "Water, water, everywhere and not a drop to drink" is widely used as an example of irony.

| *DTel* | **Further variations on** *Telegraph* **page-turning** | 31 Dec |

SIR - I still turn the pages of my *Telegraph*, without any noise, using one finger on the mouse pad of my laptop (Letters, December 17, 2010 and December 31). I like to read to it in bed in the morning before I get up, but as I am the slower reader, my wife complains about the speed with which I move through the pages, and on Saturdays reach the magazine, which is a recent and welcome addition.

2013

The Times   **Lives remembered**   1 Jan

Tony Greig

Tony Greig's combative "I intend to make them grovel" before a ball had been bowled in the Test series between England and the West Indies in 1976 (obituary, Dec 31) was answered most emphatically on the field, never more so than during the final Test at The Oval when England succumbed to two magnificent spells of bowling by Michael Holding. I attended on the Saturday, when a calypso record *Who's Grovelling Now*, which I still have, was being played and sold around the ground before play. This joyful riposte was all that was really necessary off the field of play and I like to imagine it helped Tony Greig keep in perspective the stick he got for his injudicious remarks.

DTel   **Intrusive images on television**   1 Jan

SIR - The anti-smoking images are indeed an intrusion (Letters, January 1), but who gave consent for the new series of anti-rape advertisements to be shown on television?

The Times 2 Jan

Magistrates' ages

Sir, Ronald Forrest's contention that many active citizens over the age of 70 would make excellent jurors could indeed apply equally well to extending the service of magistrates as they also retire at 70 (not 65) (letter, Dec 31); the question is how best to bring this about.

It would seem sensible to consider linking any increase in age limit to increments planned for the state pension. For magistrates, though, it has been claimed in answer to a parliamentary question that it would take them out of step with other judicial offices, reducing the number of available vacancies and thus reducing opportunities for younger people. There would be no fewer vacancies, though they might occur slightly later during a transition period, but would still be in keeping with the time candidates could expect to fill them.

Let this logical proposal be subject to a properly joined up inter-departmental review and let those other judicial offices keep in step by being included in it.

DTel **A female voice for TMS** 3 Jan

SIR - Peter Oborne need worry less than he might imagine about the BBC attempting to replace Christopher Martin-Jenkins in the *Test Match Special* team with another former pro or latest protégé from the Radio 5 Live sports desk (Comment, January 3). CMJ was one of the ball-by ball commentators and not a summariser, the usual role of former pros like Vic Marks, Geoffrey Boycott and Michael Vaughan. Whilst Jonathan Agnew and Simon Hughes are exceptions, recent home grown ball-by-ball commentators have not played first-class cricket. There are others – Radio 5 Live or not – who have been groomed to join the team and I, for one, would even welcome them being joined by the clear and knowledgeable female voice of Alison Mitchell waiting in the wings.

DTel **Wettest year 2000** 4 Jan

SIR - The news that 2000 is still just the wettest year on record (report, January 4) reminded me of my return in November that year from three years' living abroad in sunnier climes. Trapped one dark evening in my car waiting for the "extreme rainfall" to subside, I heard a budding comedian on the radio recalling that 100 years ago we ruled over a quarter of the world. "Why didn't we move?" he asked. As four of the five wettest years since 1910 have already happened this century, it looks as if we should have done.

What's Brewing **Pub of the year** 4 Jan

On receiving it, I happened to take my December copy of *What's Brewing* into the Shoulder of Mutton in Wantage, one of CAMRA's last 16 regional pubs of the year. The landlord was unaware that he had not made the final 4 until I read them out to him from the front page. Was this really the way that he should have discovered that his was not one of them?

The Times **Winter fuel payments** 7 Jan

Sir, My wife's mother was incapacitated by a stroke three years ago so badly that all her needs in a care home are fully funded under NHS continuing healthcare provision. On receipt, her entitlement to attendance allowance ceased and yet she has now received her third unnecessary winter fuel payment (letters, Jan 7). Both these last two entitlements come under the Department for Work and Pensions, which is apparently powerless to stop a payment for heating already being paid for by the Department of Health. Some changes in entitlement should not be seen as a climb-down but as a demonstration of joined up government.

DTel **Microwave uses** 8 Jan

SIR - My wife tells me that the porridge will remain in the bowl if it is not covered (Letters, January 9). I have told her that I shall continue to use the microwave to cook bacon placed between two pieces of kitchen towel paper.

The Times **More blue plaques** 8 Jan

Sir, An average of £965 for English Heritage to pay for blue plaques to commemorate people of distinction (report, Jan 7 and letter, Jan 9) does seem rather a lot when personalised replica versions are available to lesser brethren for as little as £12. I am toying with the idea of having one inscribed "Soldier, Cricketer, Man of Letters".

DTel	**Smart as in stylish**	10 Jan

SIR - Simon Watson (no relation) asks how to describe someone who is *smart* in the stylish sense of the word (Letters, January 9). I suggest that *well turned out* for men, and *fashionably dressed* for women, should fit the bill; at least for those aware of the term *pride in appearance*.

DTel	**Beverley setts**	13 Jan

SIR - I was born in Beverley when prams were prams (report, January 10) and built with large narrow wheels and suspension, giving an untroubled ride over the setts there until superseded by the ubiquitous buggy. This is an artificial problem about comfort for parents, carers and their charges, not access (Letters, January 12) or health and safety. Yorkshire men, women and children are made of sterner stuff and the setts should remain in place.

In the face of 2000 signatures and a couple of well attended marches, the East Riding Council backed down on 24 Jan and announced that the setts would be retained.

The Times   **BBC's role**   16 Jan

Sir, What on earth is the BBC doing owning *Lonely Planet?* ("Wiki dips toe into troubled waters with travel guides", Business, Jan 16).

The Times   18 Jan

"No 12 dress"

Sir, Of the 14 different orders of dress I wore during 39 years in the Army, my one-piece coveralls, (olive, No 12 dress) was the one most frequently worn when serving with troops. Never worn in the mess, they were put on with a beret and belt after breakfast (letter, Jan 17) and used as an over-garment while working on armoured vehicles. Now worn with a tweed cap for domestic tasks, it is the only item of uniform I retained for future use.

DTel   **The future of shopping**   19 Jan

SIR - Douglas Cairns says there is something exciting about a well-stocked shop and immediate purchase

(Letters, January 19). I made just such a purchase recently when buying Jonathan Agnew's *Aggers' Ashes* (published at £18.99 in 2011) for £1 from one of three "pound" shops near each other in Newbury. Offline, this looks like the future of browser-purchasing for me, with the savings made used to purchase a good shampoo from *The Gentlemen's Shop* in Hungerford.

The Times **Google and the Law** 19 Jan

Sir, Professor Thomas is right to suggest that jurors should be trusted ("Barristers google jurors during trial", Law, Jan 19). Not only did I google the judge and barristers when I was a juror last year, I googled the points of law on which we were likely to be directed as well. I found the information online in the *Crown Court Bench Book – Instructing the Jury,* printed off the relevant pages and was better informed and prepared for doing so.

Private Eye **Commentatorballs** 19 Jan

"So India win by 7 wickets with acres and acres of time left..."
PAUL ALLOTT, Sky Sports, 19 Jan 13

DTel	**Predictive text option**	24 Jan

SIR - Having a military background (Letters, January 24), I have been trained successfully by my daughters to turn predictive text off.

The Times	**Living without websites**	26 Jan

Sir, Having got to number 30 before finding the first of 7 websites listed which I have used ("The 50 top websites you can't live without", Jan 26), I am feeling rather lucky to be alive.

The Times		28 Jan

Well suited

Sir, Having visited the shop in Jermyn Street, I should like to assure your readers (letters, Jan 21, 22, 24) that the Churchill Room there has a display cabinet showing in gold lettering "Sir Winston Churchill's siren suit" and "Made exclusively by (1939-1945) Turnbull & Asser", and that it contains such a suit in green velvet.

Evening Standard 28 Jan

Deterrent value

Dr Farrell is being disingenuous when he says "for every £10 spent on the UK military, less than 4p is currently spent on conflict prevention" (Letters, January 24). Has he not heard of the concept of deterrence?

Sunday Times **Culture Section** 29 Jan

"I could be wrong", as Sir Humphrey Appleby said in the latest episode of the new **Yes, Prime Minister** (Gold), but the series is now looking more promising.

The Times **Moving on** 29 Jan

Sir, Overblown rhetoric was not the sole preserve of communism (letters, Jan 30). During the Cold War, I attended an American change of command parade at which the outgoing commander was praised for having achieved "outstanding standards of excellence".

DTel **Cracking walnuts** 31 Jan

SIR - Walnuts thrown at glass windows break up on impact leaving the glass intact (Letters, January 30, 31).

STel **Scottish referendum** 31 Jan

SIR - So the question for the referendum on Scotland's future is to be: "Should Scotland be an independent country?" This leaves unstated the fact that the United Kingdom would thereby be torn apart.

The ballot paper for the Alternative Vote in 2011 contained a statement ahead of a single question. This would transpose to: "At present, Scotland is part of the United Kingdom of Great Britain and Northern Ireland. Should Scotland be independent instead?" The Electoral Commission should include such a statement for this vote as well.

DTel **Booking early** 4 Feb

SIR - I was interested to read that Major Sir Michael Parker has booked the Morriston Opheus Choir for his funeral ("Your Majesty, I said, it's all going terribly wrong", Interview, February 4); as a brother officer I should like to be able to attend. However, I am delighted to see on the choir's website that the occasion is not yet on its list of forthcoming events.

2013

Sunday Times   **Civil options**   4 Feb

I was interested to read the news that proposals are being drawn up to allow unmarried heterosexual couples legal protection if they split up or one of them dies ("Give civil option to straight couples", February 3). Such a move would be particularly apt for never married brothers and/or sisters living together, often in the family home where they were brought up, as it would save the possibility of a survivor having to sell the house and move out in order to pay inheritance tax. I hope this aspect will be included in any policy and can survive being "backed by Nick Clegg."

The Times   **Dear, oh dear**   5 Feb

Sir, Sir Hugh Orde's attack on Lord Dear's understanding of the leadership shortcomings in the police is both unbecoming and unconvincing (letter, Feb 5). Like someone who knows the price of everything and the value of nothing, he cites qualifications as being the key indicator of the quality of the current leadership. They are just a start.

It is how those with qualifications perform that matters; and it is how few are performing well enough that has alerted the Home Secretary to seek a wider pool of, yes, suitably qualified and experienced leaders from other fields, or from abroad.

The Prime Minister's policing adviser Lord Wasserman, quoted by Sir Hugh, used a string of superlatives to describe the men and women at the top of the police service. In the words of a recent correspondent, "Well, he would, wouldn't he?", but in agreeing with him the President of the Association of Chief Police Officers is in denial.

The Oldie **Captions out of order** 8 Feb

SIR: M D Taylor makes a reasonable point in comparing unfavourably the wit and draughtsmanship of the cartoons in *Punch* of old and those in *The Oldie* (letter, March). However, the drawings will invariably be good enough to leave something to the imagination, but the captions must have a ring of credibility about them. Not so: "Take the yellow pill first, then the red, and the pink one last. Just like snooker" (page 17, March). No it isn't; black is last and the order would be red first, yellow, and then green, if black pills don't exist. My subscription remains – for now.

Private Eye **Latin Humour** 8 Feb

I laughed out loud at your piece "Clegg's son 'to go to St Cakes'"(Eye 1333, page 20), and even at the motto *"Quis paget entrat"*. What price *"Quod erat demonstrandum"*?

Thanks for letter.
Best wishes. Ed

| *DTel* | **Friends of horses** | 9 Feb |

SIR - Horse loving naval friends would appear to be made of sterner stuff, having no such sentimental aversion when it comes to the consumption of a Horse's Neck (Letters, February 9).

| *The Times* | **Changes at the bottom** | 9 Feb |

Sir, The suggestion that every patient should be allowed to have a relative or suitable friend ("a companion/helper") in hospital, as and when they wish, deserves our support (letter, February 9).

However, with the situation as it is now, it will be just as likely that the ward staff will be learning from the companion/helper as the other way around. Also, until safe staffing levels are universal, they may well see little of the staff on the more challenging wards as they are diverted to patients who have no relatives or good friends to rely on.

But as it appears from the Francis report that there are to be no changes in personnel at the top, the opportunity for such two-way learning and improvement at the bottom should be grasped to help reverse what has gone so terribly wrong.

Daily Mail	**No need to keep up**	9 Feb

Three cheers for Tom Utley for putting faith in the study from Norway which found that couples who keep pace with each other's drinking are far more likely to stick together than those who don't (Feb 7). Or should that be two cheers for him and one for Mrs U? Sharing a bottle of wine two-thirds to one-third, or having two drinks to her one is probably more the norm and has the same effect in most cases - that is if us men of the same faith are at all honest about it.

STel	**Horse-free zone**	10 Feb

SIR - John Davies from Tunbridge Wells says he has never been "disgusted" (Letter, February 10). I may be prejudiced, but I don't somehow associate the large Royal town with ready-made lasagne.

The Cricket Paper		13 Feb

Yorkshire fans saw it coming

Guy Williams is mistaken "that no one could have imagined in Victorian England that Yorkshire would become the most successful of all the English counties" - all of Yorkshire would have done.

For Brian Close and Ray Illingworth to infer that Philip Sharpe or Willie Watson have better records than Geoffrey Boycott is disingenuous. The only reason that Boycott can't squeeze in their all-time best Yorkshire XIs is because Close and Illingworth are picking them, neither of whose own records warrant inclusion.

(Instead, Michael Vaughan and Darren Gough, the only two good enough in Martyn Moxon's XI, would produce a stronger and better balanced final XI.) A similar point to one published in a letter the previous week and so edited out.

DTel **PC cigars** 14 Feb

SIR - Allan Massie is wrong to associate Sir Winston Churchill with a "fat" cigar ("Why I believe in the wisdom of pipe smoking", Comment, February 14). Always striving to be politically correct, he classified his cigars as "large", "small", "wrapped" and naked".

The Times **Tibet** 20 Feb

Sir, The long list of British signatories with historic links to Tibet going back up to 200 years (letter, Feb 20) do not seem to have considered in their suggested affirmative actions what is in them for China. Whilst they cite China as losing goodwill around the world, that is something that it will have calculated it can live with. They should focus on what China cannot live without in the next 100 years, which is unlikely to be further self-inflicted Tibetan deaths.

DTel **The light's on in rural England** 22 Feb

SIR - The Chairman of the Campaign to Protect Rural England seems unaware of one of the laws of nimbyism: that one man's well-designed, higher density urban development is another man's town cramming (Letters, February 22), whatever the natural light incident on it.

The Times 23 Feb

Reasonable juries

Sir, There is an alternative to the suggestions (letter, Feb 22) to having judges sit with magistrates and providing all juries with access to a legal adviser. Last year I was in a jury alongside a barrister who helped with the judge's written and oral directions. Now that barristers or solicitor advocates are no longer exempt, it should not be beyond HM Courts & Tribunal Service to summons them to serve on each jury. Judging by the reactions in our case, there would seem to be benefits all round.

The Times **Acting out sentencing** 24 Feb

Sir, Your former editor, William Rees-Mogg, "was renowned among staff for insisting that no sentence needed more than 15 words" (leading article, Dec 31). Is Matthew Parris's 154-word sentence ("Long live shopping. But the shop is dead", Opinion, Feb 23) the result of what happens when the editor is only "acting"?

Daily Telegraph 24 Feb

The Royal family's frugal living arrangements (P)

SIR - Vicky Woods says you can't put an electric fire in a bathroom (Comment, February 23) - but you can. Ours has a circular ring-coil element around the ceiling light fitting, which warms the room when the central heating is not on.

STel **Our stamps are special too** 27 Feb

SIR - There are still 10 of the 12 sets of special stamps left to brighten the day in 2013, including one of portraits of the Queen which will not feature an additional Queen's head (Letters, February 24). Unfortunately, some counter staff seem reluctant to offer them, and promotional material at post offices has all but disappeared. However, those seeking them out will find the designs, **especially the butterflies, to be** a colourful match for anything coming from abroad.

The Times **Not that intelligent** 28 Feb

Sir, What kind of corporate knowledge is there in the BBC now when an Oxford graduate newscaster can read out that Private First Class Bradley Manning is an army intelligence officer? I despair.

The Cricketer Mar issue

Tony Greig remembered

I attended on the Saturday of the 1976 Test at The Oval, when England succumbed to two magnificent spells of bowling by Michael Holding. A calypso record 'Who's Grovelling Now?', which I still have, was being played and sold around the ground before play. This joyful riposte was all that was really necessary off the field of play and I like to imagine it helped Tony Greig keep in perspective the stick he got for his injudicious remarks.

The Times　　　　　**Eastleigh by-election**　　　　3 Mar

Sir, In saying that Nigel Farage, the UKIP leader, must be kicking himself for not standing in the Eastleigh by-election, your leading article (Mar 2) does a disservice to their candidate, Diane James. The eccentric leader would just as likely have put off some potential voters as the highly credible Ms James was able to attract them, and not necessarily from the same rival party. What the close result has done is reminded us that first-past-the-post leaves no place for losers; and it has shown that no party or candidate can afford to be despised by default on the doorstep.

The Times　　　　　**Real mathematicians**　　　　6 Mar

Sir, Before GCSEs, maths was segregated at 'O' level into Elementary Maths and Additional Maths, which included real maths in the form of calculus and coordinate geometry, essential later for studying the design of buildings, bridges and all machines (letters, Feb 18, Mar 5). I don't recall any of us reading science or engineering at university in those days giving up time from our attempts to arrest the decline of real ale to attend remedial classes in maths.

DTel **Catholic priests in Scotland** 10 Mar

SIR - It must be reassuring for many to read (Report, March 9) that there were some supposedly celibate priests in the Catholic Church in Scotland at risk of exposure for being "out of control sexually" who are heterosexual; but that they were having trouble managing their sexuality would seem to be an unfortunate turn of phrase to use about them.

DTel **Lady in red** 11 Mar

SIR - One place where red pillar-boxes, phone boxes and double-decker buses can still be guaranteed to be seen together is in Victoria, the capital of British Columbia, Canada.

The Times 12 Mar

History of the Commonwealth

Sir, The Balfour Declaration (of 1926), which Libby Purves quotes from (Mar 11), was not about "54 nations, large and small, rich and poor", but about the United

Kingdom and the Dominions being "autonomous Communities within the British Empire". It accepted the growing political and diplomatic independence of Canada, Australia, New Zealand, Newfoundland, the Union of South Africa and the Irish Free State in the years after the First World War.

Today, the Commonwealth — of independent sovereign states — is less "united by a common allegiance to the Crown" than by voluntary association, five members having their own monarchies (Brunei, Lesotho, Malaysia, Swaziland and Tonga) and a number being republics. Not surprisingly, then, implacable opposition to discrimination against lesbian, gay, bisexual and transgender people has had to be rooted in "other grounds" in its new Charter, for the Queen, as Head of the Commonwealth, to speak in support of it (letter, Mar 12).

Sunday Times **Culture Section** 13 Mar

It is a travesty that the title **Food & Drink** (BBC 2) has been taken from its previous incarnation, when bitter would no more have had body than wine taste of hops. The host must rue the day he got involved with this poor series and should decline another to save his reputation.

The Times **One for the Green Party** 14 Mar

Sir, My own favourite organisational taunt concerns a woodpeckers' party in Sherwood Forest ("Heady Ed makes Dave's fizz fall flat", News, Mar 14).

TheTimes **Freedom to blow the whistle** 16 Mar

Sir, Healthy rivalry between this country's quality newspapers must be a good thing, but Matthew Parris is being more provocative than usual in declaring of the MPs' expenses scandal – tantalisingly exposed by *The Daily Telegraph* - that "the whole story was uncovered through stolen personal records" (Opinion, Mar 16). No criminal activity has been proven against the whistleblower and, in the end, it was the Freedom of Information Act which hoisted MPs by their own petard.

THE WIT AND WISDOM OF AN ORDINARY SUBJECT

Times Feedback **Correction** 18 Mar

Madam, I hope you will feel that a correction should be published about the caption to the photograph under "The day the Queen put the Prime Minister in his place" (Mar 16). Point 4 in the panel states that Prince Albert was the Queen's grandfather; he was her great-great-grandfather. However, the picture looks as if it might actually be of his first son, Prince Edward Albert, Prince of Wales, (later King Edward VII). If so then he was her great-grandfather.

Dear Mr Watson,

Thank you for writing in about this, and please accept our apologies for a stupid error. We will run a correction in tomorrow's paper.

With best wishes,

Rose Wild
Feedback editor, The Times

2013

Evening Standard   19 Mar

London's landmarks

Battersea Power Station cannot possibly be "London's favourite landmark" ("Power to the people", March 18), for which there are many more worthy contenders. It would, though, be reasonable to describe the landmark as "long-standing".

J M C Watson

The Times   **Triple wedding**   20 Mar

Sir, The triple engagement announcements of the Ramsey siblings in *The Times* must be a rare occurrence, but it is not unique (letter, Mar 18). On 29 April 1981 the newspaper announced the engagements of three Morgan sisters. This was followed in September that year with a triple wedding in France at which their father took each daughter up the aisle in turn and a large outdoor reception. Whilst that occasion was not recorded in *The Times,* their marriages were marked for the guests by a special souvenir edition of the *International Herald Tribune* with the wedding invitation replicated as the front page. Perhaps against the odds for our time, all three couples remain happily married with three children each, the first two being born to the younger wives on the same day; and I still have my copy of the newspaper memento.

DTel **Rote learning** 20 Mar

SIR - I write as a non-academic to suggest that Professor Brassey and 99 other academics (Letter, March 20) are mistaken in their belief that "the mountain of data" will not develop children's ability to think. It is precisely because they know from rote learning, for example that 7 x 8 is 56 and how to spell "right" and "wrong", that they are free to develop that thinking and not waste it on what they should know through instant recall. We must not allow rote learning to be described as "dumbing down", but as an essential tool to bring our children back up to standard in our own eyes as well as internationally.

DTel **More rote please** 21 Mar

SIR - I hope that all one hundred of the academics writing about the dangers posed by Michael Gove's new National Curriculum (Letters, March 20) will have read the dissection of their misguided antipathy towards rote learning in the excellent article by Harry Mount ("Children can't think if they don't know the facts" March 21). However, I fear the real danger is that they will not wish to learn from it and apply some "critical understanding" of their own for the benefit of pupils and teachers in their spheres of influence. When will we ever learn, even if not by rote?

| *DTel* | ** *DTel* **journalists' punctuation** **
is alive and well | 23 Mar |

SIR - Robert Tapsfield cannot remember when he last saw a piece of journalism with a semi-colon in it (Letters, March 23). I do hope he had time to read the leading article on the same page and the articles by Charles Moore and Vicki Woods on the page opposite, all of which used it. The style of Damian Thompson's column there had less need for the semi-colon, but he made ample use of the dash and the colon instead. Sign-writers are another matter altogether.

| *The Times* | **Epic final** | 27 Mar |

Sir, How fortunate that the biblical epic *The Greatest Story Ever Told* (1965) did not achieve greater critical acclaim: "Jesus Christ! the book was better" (*The Sunday Times Guide to Movies on Television,* 1973 and 1980*)*. Had it done so, it would have been an obvious candidate to join Barry Norman's list of best epic movies for consideration (letter, Mar 27) - and a

THE WIT AND WISDOM OF AN ORDINARY SUBJECT

natural favourite - to be named the greatest story ever filmed, putting paid to any future speculation.

DTel　　　　**Fooling around with Easter**　　29 Mar

SIR - As Lord President of the Council, here is something else which is not broken for Nick Clegg to try and interfere with: setting Easter, by bringing forward an Order in Council waiting to do so since 1928 (Letters, March 29). Interestingly, the only occasion when "the first Sunday after the second Saturday" is not also the second Sunday in April is when April Fools' Day falls on a Sunday. As it falls on Easter Monday this year, April 1 next year would seem be a suitable date for him to try.

The Times　　　**Cleaning-in-confidence**　　1 Apr

Sir, Would that I had been able to contact the cleaner on my mother's ward (letter, Apr 1) after she was admitted to hospital following a fall last week. On Good Friday, I had to travel 220 miles to get past the ward staff who were unable to discuss her predicament on the telephone due to rules of "confidentiality". Thank goodness I was back at home by Saturday night, as my wife's mother died on Easter morning.

2013

At this point, (to paraphrase the author of The Flashman Papers, *the late George MacDonald Fraser) the first packet of* Wit and Wisdom *ends abruptly.*

EXTRAS

THE WIT AND WISDOM OF AN ORDINARY SUBJECT

The Times 2 May 09

A long dismissal

Sir, I wonder if the following dismissal (Sport, April 30) from the Hampshire v Sussex match constitutes, in terms of characters, one of the longest in county cricket? C C Benham c Hamilton-Brown b Martin-Jenkins, 1
CHRISTOPHER COLLINS
Alton, Hampshire

The Times **How's this?** 4 May 09

Sir, A quick glance amongst the obvious candidates reveals that *J Birkenshaw c Ingelby–Mackenzie b Shackelton , 0,* exceeds Christopher Collins' suggestion (letter, May 2) by two characters and the very next dismissal listed in the same match (Hampshire v Leicestershire, May 1962), *J van Geloven c Ingelby-Mackenzie b Sainsbury, 3,* by one character, each without the involvement of a second double-barrelled name.

However, I have only had instant access to *Wisden Almanacks* going back to 1962. Dismissals involving H D G Leveson Gower (Surrey), K S Ranjitsinhji, K S Duleepsinhji (both Sussex) and the Nawabs of Pataudi (Worcestershire and Sussex) would seem to be productive sources in other eras; and if A C D Ingelby-Mackenzie and J P Fellows-Smith (Northamptonshire) were involved in each other's dismissals, then those might be unbeatable.

The Times   *4 May 09*

Long dismissals in Indian cricket

Sir, Christopher Collins (letter, May 2) looks for the longest dismissal in terms of characters. I cannot answer for county cricket but the match between Andhra Pradesh and Kerala — reported in The Times of November 17, 1990 — has this line: Chamundeswaranagh c Balasabramaniam b Anantapadmanabhan 2
MICHAEL OPENSHAW
London NW3

DTel   **Mexican drinks - sangrita**   13 Jun 09
(Weekend)

Dear Mr Ray,

I am sure you would wish to know that the chaser you describe in your article in *The Daily Telegraph* today is in fact called "sangrita" and not sangria, which is of course something quite different.

I shall try Simon Warneford's recipe and call in at the Merkaba when I am in Brighton the week after next.

You might also be interested to know that Herradura Blanco, if you had the real thing and not an export version, is 46% for the Mexican market and is "para los hombres"!

Yours sincerely,

Malcolm Watson
British Defence Attaché, Mexico City, 1997-2000

Dear Mr Watson,   *13 Jun 09*

Thank you so much for your email. It was kind of you to write in.

I've been fuming all morning having seen the paper. You may or may not know that all our copy is subbed in Australia these days and for some reason best known to them, the Aussie subs decided to alter my text from 'sangrita' to 'sangria'. It makes me look even more of an idiot than I already am and I'm hopping!

Simon Warneford is going to give me stick too, I just know it! Sigh.

Anyway, I hope you enjoy the cocktails at the Merkaba.

Very best, Jonathan

EXTRAS

The Oldie **Competition No 135** 18 Feb 11

The annual *bouts-rimés*. A poem of 16 lines with these words as the rhymes in the order given: fate, time, great, rhyme, low, best, show, rest, raise, filled, yesterdays, build, these, between, sees, unseen.*

What it would be to know our fate
Before the Lord calls: "Time."
We could be doing something great,
Without reason or rhyme.

In that case we need not feel low,
For we'll be at our best.
So we could put on quite a show
Before we're laid to rest.

But if that fate a problem raise,
The days must still be filled.
Till they become our yesterdays,
We have a life to build.

The choices may not be just these;
Worse fates could lie between.
Perhaps what e'er the good Lord sees
Is better left unseen.

*Later revealed to be the first half of Longfellow's "The Builders"

THE WIT AND WISDOM OF AN ORDINARY SUBJECT

DTel **But what does it taste like?** 22 Apr 11
(Weekend)

Dear Miss Moore,

I enjoy reading your column and about the wines you've enjoyed - last week one of them was Campillo Rioja Gran Reserva 1978. I am highly unlikely ever to pay £42 for a bottle of wine, but I would like to read and imagine what it tastes like; not a word of your description mentioned taste!

Yours sincerely,

Malcolm Watson

Hello, *27 Apr 11*

The autumn leaf bit was about the taste....I tend to think that with these expensive wines you undermine them when you try to pin them down so much. What's magical isn't so much the flavour as the way they play, it's like having an orchestra instead of a single instrument so you get layers and nuances that you can sit back and enjoy. Finesse and detail too.

Victoria

EXTRAS

The Oldie **Competition 156** 27 Sep 12

A publisher's letter pointing out to a now famous author, perhaps a little crassly, some of the deficiencies of a well-known book.
Maximum 150 words.

Dear Mr MacDonald Fraser,

I am returning your manuscript "Flashman", about the bully from *Tom Brown's Schooldays*. The introductory note explaining that you have edited the first packet from some papers discovered in 1965 during a sale of household furniture in Leicestershire may fool some Americans, but not a military publishing house like ours.

For a start, the 11th Light Dragoons would have regarded an officer who went to school at Rugby as far too plebian to be one of them. Also, I am puzzled why you think that the 1st Anglo-Afghan War could have any possible interest for the modern-day reader.

I congratulate you, though, on the exceptional historical footnotes which accompany the script. These I see as the basis of a standard textbook and would be happy to recommend an academic publisher.

In the meantime, I wish you continued good fortune as deputy editor of the *Glasgow Herald*.

The Oldie   February 2013

The Old Un's diary

Double-take Five

In early December, the *Daily Telegraph* announced the birthday of jazz musician Dave Brubeck. The only slight problem was that on the opposite page it published Brubeck's obituary. Eagle-eyed Malcolm Watson spotted this gaffe and wrote a letter to the *Telegraph's* editor pointing out that Brubeck's age of 92 appeared to be slightly exaggerated. Although the broadsheet has published a number of Watson's letters on other subjects, this one failed to make the cut…

THE LAST WORD

"And when I'm finally called, by the Great Architect, and they say 'What did you do?', I shall just bring out my book and I shall say 'Here you are mate, add that lot up.' "

Tony Hancock, *The Blood Donor*

ACKNOWLEDGEMENTS

This book has been self-published, which as the term implies, you have to do it yourself and that is what I have done. However, there are a few others who have been instrumental in setting me off along this path and who have encouraged me to get to the end of it.

Andy and Clare MacInnes who pruned my first published letter of 2010 and thus enthused me into trying again. Lee West and Robert Deighton, followers of the *Telegraph* and *Times* letters pages respectively for spotting my contributions and suggesting that they would appeal to a wider audience; Robert Deighton again, Alistair and Nicola Irwin, and 'Wilf' Hyde-Smith for reading through draft manuscripts and urging publication; and Kate Fenton for suggesting Lulu.com for online self-publishing.

Other correspondents' letters from *The Times* and emails from the staff are reproduced by kind permission of Ian Brunskill, Editor, Letters, Obituaries & Register. Other letters from *The Daily Telegraph* are reproduced by kind permission of the correspondents themselves. The email from *The Sunday Times* is reproduced by kind permission of Parin Janmohamed, Letters Editor. The letter to *The Guardian*, also published in *The Week*, is reproduced by kind permission of Helen Wilson, their Commercial Content Sales Manager. Fiona Duncan of *The Sunday Telegraph (Discovery Section)* has kindly permitted publication of her email to me. So too have Victoria Moore and Jonathan Ray, current and former wine correspondents of *The Daily Telegraph*. Extracts from *The Oldie* magazine appear by kind permission of James Pembroke, its publisher.

The quote by Tony Hancock from *The Blood Donor* has been included by kind permission of Ray Galton and Alan Simpson.

Finally, I am indebted to three acknowledged exponents of the written word in their respective fields for their enticing forewords and to another, Lord Dear in his for his ringing endorsement on the back cover.

A PDF version can be obtained at www.lulu.com

The picture on the cover is taken from a cartoon drawn by Bill Tidy (see page 139) during a cricket match in Germany against The Lord's Taverners in 1981.

ABOUT THE SUBJECT

Malcolm Watson was born in Beverley in the East Riding of Yorkshire and educated at Oundle and the Royal Military Academy Sandhurst, being commissioned into The Queen's Own Hussars; and at the Royal Military College of Science Shrivenham, from where he obtained a degree in Aeromechanical Engineering. He was in the Army for 39 years, serving at various times in England and Northern Ireland, and abroad in Cyprus, Hong Kong, West Germany, West Berlin, Washington DC and Mexico City, where as the defence attaché he was also accredited to Belize and Cuba. He has made 10 military parachute jumps and flown 35 hours in a Piper Cherokee. He played and watched more cricket than was thought possible for a serviceman; he has been a member of Yorkshire County Cricket Club for 50 years and MCC for 34. He enjoys acting the fool and has taken part in a number of reviews on stage and elsewhere. His only serious and non-speaking part, to date, was playing King George IV at his Coronation in the Berlin Military Tattoo. He is interested in everything except classical music, Shakespeare and Greek mythology. He is married to Jane and they have 3 daughters, Anna, Edwina and Fenella.

"…he will speak his mind whenever the occasion warrants it (and perhaps some when it does not!)…"
Extract from a Regular Army Confidential Report.